Twelve Principles *of* Effective Parenting

Surviving the Tween Years

David Celio, PhD

PAULIST PRESS
New York/Mahwah, NJ

Cover design by Joy Taylor
Book design by Lynn Else

Library of Congress Cataloging-in-Publication Data

Celio, David.
Twelve principles of effective parenting : surviving the tween years / David Celio.
p. cm.
Includes bibliographical references (p.).
ISBN 978-0-8091-4683-3 (alk. paper)
1. Parent and teenager. 2. Parenting. I. Title.
HQ799.15.C44 2011
649′.125—dc22

2010029157

Published by Paulist Press
997 Macarthur Boulevard
Mahwah, New Jersey 07430

www.paulistpress.com

Printed and bound in the
United States of America

Table of Contents

Prologue

There is a weather forecaster here in rainy Seattle who likes to say that on some days any fool can predict the weather, and on other days only a fool would try. It is with this same sense of humility that I approached the task of writing a book about parenting. At times parents say the job of parenting is easy and in these moments they feel some sense of expertise. At other moments they say they can be totally befuddled and reluctantly admit they have lost their way in responding to their children. I wanted to share what I have learned from over thirty years of helping families in my clinical practice plus what I applied to my own family. Take courage. We lived through it and survived. You can too. My wife and I raised five children, sent them all to a public elementary, then to a private middle school, and finally to a Jesuit high school in preparation for a successful college experience. We bonded with other thoughtful parents and solved numerous problems along the way, mostly because we prepared ourselves in the ways described in this book. Back then we met with similarly minded parents in a kind of loose support group. We all wanted success for our children. We were mostly two-career families, and we all faced personal and academic challenges at home and at school. Because I was a clinical psychologist with a specialty in working with families, I was able to give some useful advice in a number of situations. One day a dad said to me, "You know, you should write all this down so other parents can benefit from your advice and our experience." That was years ago, but the thought stuck in my mind, and when I recently had a career transition, I used the time to do just that. That is how this book came to be.

It is easy to become a parent and difficult to be a parent. The years of daily commitment and effort can be exhilarating but wearing in time and energy. The more children we have, moreover, the more complex the task. It is no wonder we see only a few brave families of four to six children anymore. But the daunting challenges of child-raising can be made easier if we grasp several important principles, articulate them, and apply them on a continuing basis. These principles are outlined in this book. Unlike other books about parenting, I have tried to emphasize these principles rather than relying primarily on storytelling so that you can think carefully about the wisdom offered by experienced parents. If you do not agree with what we found to be successful, I encourage you to discover what works well for you. Above all, think the problem through.

The metaphor of parenting children is captured in how we teach a child to ride a bicycle. We envision the child riding her bicycle skillfully, safely, and ready to explore the world. But teaching these complex skills can best be accomplished in stages: learning to balance, steer, and navigate all at once requires understanding, coordination, and lots of practice. A parent begins by selecting an appropriate bicycle, explaining what it takes to ride the bike, and teaching the skills in stages appropriate to the child's age and maturity. In the beginning, the parent will literally hold onto the bike as the child sits on the seat with her hands on the handle bars. The parent guides the child along a path while instructing how to balance, peddle, steer, and brake. It takes practice and correction. When the child can balance and steer, the parent will lessen his hold and give the child more freedom to pilot, continuing to do so as the child gradually attains mastery of each stage of riding. Then, with faith in God as much as in teaching skill, the parent will let the child go and she will ride alone for a short distance. It is an exhilarating moment to behold as the child rides independently. But we know more practice is needed. There will be more to learn, and there will likely be spills and crashes along the way to establishing full competence. The parent will be careful not to expect too much too soon. The child will have to learn the rules of safe driving for herself and demonstrate mastery in increasingly complex traffic. With such instruction and practice, the child will master this competency fully over time.

Note the role of the parent as teacher. Those qualities we admire in teachers are also required of parents: caring, dedication, effective listening, encouragement, limit-setting, and praise. If we are thoughtful in how we present our messages to our children, then our wishes and dreams of success for our children are more likely to come true.

David Celio, PhD
Seattle, Washington

Introduction

A mother I know describes her life as resembling that of a Chinese acrobat. You know the kind—she spins rings around each knee, balances saucers on poles she holds with each hand, and guides a ball on her forehead. And on national holidays she is expected to sing the national anthem while doing all this. This mother has a demanding career that includes continuing professional preparation, three distinctly different children, a hardworking husband, and a home to manage that requires daily meal preparation and delivery, washing and sorting clothes, and other activities to keep the county health department at bay. Never mind the garden or house projects. She admits at times it feels like a race to the grave, but through it all she maintains that she would not trade her life for another. She loves her job and family, but she says it is extremely hard raising children in this stressful context. She admits feeling guilty that with both her and her husband working and sharing household duties, they do not get to do the fun activities they used to. It is the contemporary dilemma of conflicting aspirations, expectations, and limitations. The best we can do, she agrees, is to define what we really value in life and practice regimens that move us toward these goals.

The driving assumption of this book is that we as parents want a fulfilling and happy life for our children, and we are willing to invest the necessary time and energy to produce this outcome. Parenting is rewarding but unrelenting work. We read occasional reports that marital satisfaction is diminished after the birth of children, but upon closer examination we find these ratings are usually based on an individual's assessment of fewer opportunities for good times as they were experienced in youth.[1] Absent is their assessment of contributing and witnessing the growth and success of those we love, that vicarious fulfillment of life's dreams that have motivated parents since time immemorial. If we include the happiness and satisfaction of seeing our children succeed, then parenting becomes not the cause of diminished happiness but a significant enhancement to our satisfaction and meaning in life.

In over thirty years of child and family practice, I have been told by some people that they carefully planned to have children, while others admitted it was "the next thing to do" after marriage. Upon further reflection, however, even those who see parenting as a normal urge to extend their lineage are doing more than meeting a cultural expectation: it is their unique contribution to make society a better place. It is their very personal effort to raise children who hopefully will add productive work to our communities, who will lead lives of personal integrity, and who will display a sincere caring for others. Raising such productive and caring children is a worthy goal, and we should try to support each other to produce a better society.

We have already referred to parents as teachers. Parents have the most profound influence on their children and can benefit from the experience of other successful parents. That is why we have tried to distill from the mass of literature and discussion twelve principles that can provide parents with a starting place to think about or review what direction would be helpful.

We cannot do it alone. By carefully selecting an achieving public school, an innovative charter school, a selective private school, or a parish Catholic school, we as parents are giving our children a special gift: a sustained educational opportunity that parallels our teaching at home and thus better prepares our children for life's challenges. Each family should reflect on the values it wants to live by and then find a school that is congruent with these values. Experienced parents who inspired this book especially advocated the following characteristics:

1. Moral values: we think carefully about what it takes to be our best selves, the values we admire and strive for in personal development. We strive for characteristics we admire or look to our faith to find direction. We recognize that caring for others is of collateral importance to self-development, and as parents we hope to inspire our children by modeling these virtues.
2. Hard work: we value the satisfaction of investing time and effort to achieve a result to be proud of, and celebrate with pride a job well done.
3. Socialization: we want to teach our children to control their impulses that interfere with fulfilling responsibilities and caring for others. This process involves learning the discipline to stay on track as well as to remember that our behavior affects others.
4. Encouragement: this is our preferred tool to foster ambition and to expect success. We praise appropriately and maintain a positive attitude that our children will succeed.
5. Help: we want help to be available. We realize we must do more than merely expect our children to succeed. We must give them the tools and teach them how to use them. We provide daily supervision, and as the child develops increasing responsibility and competence, we gradually withdraw the daily support until they are fully competent.
6. Community service: we expect our children to contribute to the community. So much of our focus

> is on the child's individual achievement that we must keep in mind how his contributions fit into the larger pattern of society.

The challenge for parents, then, is to find a school environment that supports the values we advocate in our families. Sometimes we live in communities where this congruence of values is present, and merely enrolling our child in the local school satisfies this goal. In other communities, particularly larger school districts, parents take a more activist stance and search out the styles of various teachers or schools. Parents should be concerned with finding a good fit between a teacher and their child, and helpful principals do their best to respond to parental questions before teacher assignment. Where parents choose a private or Catholic school, there is often more concern for a good match, and sensitive administrators weigh teacher comments in making these assignments. Discussing these assignments before final decisions are made is a positive sign of the school's responsiveness.

A particularly promising development in recent years has been the emergence of charter schools, publicly funded schools with varying focus depending on the local community. Paul Hill, PhD, of the Center for the Reinvention of Public Education,[2] has noted that charter schools as a whole compare favorably to and bring to memory the aspirations of Catholic schools of the last century that successfully educated immigrant populations in America. Hill describes characteristics similar to what we have advocated for family/school values, starting with the hard work of a demanding intellectual climate emphasizing basic skills, and a centripetal curriculum that all students must master. In these schools, teachers work together to coordinate instruction for each child and pay close attention to student progress so no one falls far behind. The school climate is strongly managed to maintain order, and rules are upheld so learning can take place without distraction. The moral values of helping others and respecting cultural differences are emphasized in order to prepare students for today's multicultural world. Finally, help in the form of guidance is consistently available for students to succeed in academic and social situations. Teachers model school values and the older students are expected to set examples for the younger students. Principals and teachers work to inspire as well as to teach these values.

This book focuses on the middle school years, approximately grades six through eight in most parts of the country, for very good reasons. Recent research has confirmed what many experienced parents already discuss in the aisles of grocery stores or at sports practices or games: these early teen years are filled with changes and challenges that have become more complex as society has changed. Situations that most children once knew little about until the late teen years have become familiar to preteens as TV, movies, the Internet, and music have exposed young people to behaviors and choices that no girl or boy of thirteen or fourteen is prepared to handle. It would undoubtedly be best if we could screen out all these influences until our children are ready to deal with them, but that is very difficult to do. Instead, as parents, we accept the challenge of teaching our children how to grow into responsible, caring, and successful young adults in today's world.

In the following sections you will be asked to reflect on various ways you can enrich and support your child's education. We begin by addressing your goals and wishes for your child. Parents[3] should discern their own values and discuss with their partners what results they would like to see from the child's education. Establish the track you desire for your child so you will know when he is on or off it. Sometimes adult retreats sponsored by a parish provide for this reflection, but all that is necessary is the opportunity to define your expectations in dialogue with your partner and the willingness to continue this dialogue. By clarifying your goals, it will also make communication with your child's teacher easier.

We include a section on child development. Although this topic extends far beyond the brief message we provide here, there are some basic principles you should be aware of. It makes a difference to your child when you present messages he can fully understand. The middle years of childhood are a time of amazing physical, intellectual, and emotional growth, so it is important to become familiar with these changes.

Listening to your child is an essential part of good communication, and we want to point out some elements of effective listening as well as of sending clear messages. Staying involved with your child's activities is fundamental to good communication. This can be difficult when we have jobs to go to, meals to shop for and prepare, bills to pay, and houses to clean. Nonetheless, we would be missing the most important part of our child's experience if we failed to maintain effective communication. An important part of good communication, moreover, is our ability to know our own emotional strengths and liabilities, particularly if circumstances in our child's life remind us of our own experiences.

We emphasize the day-to-day supervision of your child's life. Your child does not grow up on automatic pilot: you will need to guide her based on your values and expectations. This means you should advocate for your child; attempt to establish a supportive environment in which to learn; monitor her friends; and remain active in keeping her on track with your expectations.

Much is said about the role of discipline in raising a child. We define discipline in this book as teaching your child the limits, boundaries, and expectations of society. We advocate a behavioral rather than a punitive approach, and this includes parents' setting a good example as well as providing clear instruction for the goals you set for your child.

With a clearly articulated set of values and expectations, a basic knowledge of child development, a good degree of self-awareness, effective communication with your child, and good management of your child's behavior, you will be ideally ready to discuss your child with his teacher. You will want to establish a partnership with the teacher for the mutual goal of the child's positive progress. Hopefully, the school year will be a collaborative effort where your child will face challenges with support and feel encouraged to achieve and grow emotionally as well as intellectually.

In several ways we have been addressing the growth of your child's self-esteem. So many indices of success in our society are correlated with high self-esteem that it is appropriate that we extend significant effort in this direction. Children learn more effectively, develop more confident personalities, and display more social effectiveness when they feel positive about themselves. With good self-esteem, they can better understand confusing questions of prejudice, gender identity, and the temperaments of their peers.

Next, we turn to the unique stresses our daughters face and, in particular, the dramatic physical and emotional changes they experience in their middle years. Parents should be prepared for the number of problems unique to girls. Boys, too, experience special challenges during the middle years, so we then attempt to sensitize parents to the struggles boys encounter as they emerge toward manhood. Then we confront the problems of sibling rivalry or, more generally, maintaining a harmonious family during these turbulent years.

Chapter 11 addresses a topic that has become a contemporary problem: Internet safety. The easy access to technology has contributed to remarkable educational progress and social opportunities. But this open door has also led to exposure to questionable information and even potential exploitation. There are risks we see every day, and we are obliged to teach our children strategies to remain safe. We include a chapter by Dr. Angela Celio Doyle, of the University of Chicago department of psychiatry, on how to meet the challenges of using the Internet safely.

Inevitably, we will confront problems of academic, emotional, or physical behavior. We devote a section to common problems families encounter. Fortunately, a number of families before you have experienced problems and solved them. They have added to the social capital of your school by sharing their experiences in problem solving. Some of these problems are emotional disorders you would do well to become familiar with. Your child may come to suffer from one of these problems, or you may encounter one of your child's classmates who demonstrate certain symptoms. You will want to recognize these difficulties.

Finally, we emphasize the primary importance of family. We feel it is essential for families to provide mutual support and understanding throughout the years in the face of the many challenges the student will face. Families provide a sense of identity and belonging as well as protection and support. We emphasize the support of marriage and keeping relationships vital.

In summary, we feel a thorough familiarization with these topics will begin to prepare families for the wonderful opportunity of education in the middle school years and bring parents' goals and wishes for their children closer to reality.[4]

The Twelve Principles of Effective Parenting

1. You and your spouse should unite to define the goals and expectations you hold for your children in their education and social development.
2. The middle school years represent a period of enormous physical and emotional growth. Parents need to be aware of these patterns and encourage healthy habits to respond to these dramatic changes.
3. Effective listening is the key to understanding your child and how to motivate him. Awareness of one's own feelings can help a parent to consider how to express his message.
4. Parents and teachers should form a supportive alliance to benefit the child.
5. Parents would be wise to become familiar with the unique problems girls face as they try to succeed socially and academically. Parents should engage their daughters sensitively in thought-provoking discussions to keep them on the right path for success.
6. Parents need to become familiar with the boy's struggle to believe in himself as a young man and should be sure to teach him alternative ways to feel confident and competent.
7. Parents should convey the idea that sufficient love and attention are available for each child. Competi-

tion means to do one's personal best and support other family members' best efforts as well. As a family, you are all in life's struggles together.

8. Disciplinary opportunities provide teachable moments in which parents can supportively reinforce those values they have defined as leading to success.
9. Parents would do well to broaden their understanding of children's problem behaviors, learn how to listen, and effectively intervene so over time the child develops internal controls, a conscience.
10. Parents may encounter any number of serious problems in their child or among their child's friends. It is helpful to understand what they mean, what conditions lead to these manifestations, and how best to intervene. Professional help is always an option.
11. Families can control some stress in their lives with preventive thinking and careful vigilance regarding Internet use.
12. Maintaining a healthy family means attending not only to parenting, but achieving a satisfying career and an enriching life as a couple.

CHAPTER 1

Getting on the Right Track

Principle: You and your spouse should unite to define the goals and expectations you hold for your children in their education and social development.

Robert, Mae, and Justin

Robert and Mae own a busy restaurant, and sending their son Justin to Martin Luther King School represents an increase in educational expectations for this hard-working family. After Justin's school day in the seventh grade, Mae wants Justin to come to the restaurant and sit in a quiet room to do his homework and read. Robert wants him to stay busy with the many restaurant chores they must do: fold napkins, polish the tableware, stack the menus, and sweep the floor. Mae and Robert disagree and argue about how Justin should be spending his time.

What should they do?

Time seems to go by so quickly. Just days ago your child was a toddler and now he is beginning middle school. You will likely feel confident that in choosing a school consistent with your family values you are headed in the right direction, but it is important for you and your spouse to determine exactly what your expectations are. Take the time to discuss with your spouse just what you are looking for in sending your child to school.

Most parents expect an excellent academic preparation. Already parents can envision high school, college, and some kind of career for their child. Upon reflection parents can see that there are many paths that are possible and that success is dependent on a number of conditions that align positively. Most families begin with maintaining a secure and stable family environment from which the child can concentrate on the challenges he will face in school. For parents this means providing a quiet place for their child to read and do homework, and keeping adult concerns out of the child's way. It means giving the child positive attention and encouragement in his schoolwork and even in solving problems when he has trouble understanding his teacher. It means developing his confidence in himself.

This encouragement extends beyond the challenges of the classroom. Your child will be making new friends and will be interacting with classmates on the playground, in sports, and in extracurricular activities. You can have a part in developing his social skills as he selects and encounters other children from different backgrounds and families. Your child will be making a significant transition from your family life with its unique rules and expectations to a much larger arena involving many more children and an entirely new set of rules. By attending school he will have to enlarge his social repertoire and learn how to adapt to an entirely new situation. Continued discussion with him about day-to-day problems will help him understand what new expectations are ahead of him.

In discussing expectations with your partner you should define the values you expect your child to develop. You have chosen a school consistent with your family values, so you should be sure you are familiar with how these values are being taught and discuss them with your child. Your own example and your guidance at home can reinforce these values.

One of your beginning points will be going over the school's handbook (either in text or online) with your child. Your child should know the "dos" and "don'ts" and understand why the school expects these behaviors. School rules have been carefully thought out for the children's success in academic, social, and spiritual directions. The management of a large number of children, moreover, requires setting firm boundaries and limits to absolutely free expression. This is the social contract necessary to run the school and, ultimately, for the child to adapt to society as a whole. It is part of good citizenship.

When you spend time reviewing school rules with your child, you will discover where he needs additional preparation. Is he a good listener so that when his teacher gives him instruction he will hear it? Does he have an appropriate attention span for his grade so he can maintain concentration? Does he have the physical skill to perform the required tasks in the classroom or on the playground? Can he be patient when others take their turns? Can he think for himself and make good choices? Does he have enough information about his name, address, and phone number to be safe? Does he know how to reach you in case of an emergency? These are some of the questions you can review with your child in a supportive, helpful way.

On occasion, you and your spouse may discover you have differences of opinion about expectations for your child or about methods you might use to achieve your goals. Often these differences reflect your own personal experiences and preferences. It is important to explore these differences and to challenge yourself about how your child will benefit. One commonly experienced disagreement concerns methods of discipline. Some parents believe in an authoritarian style of parenting, expecting obedience without much explanation. These parents refer to children's comments as "backtalk." Other parents adopt a more permissive style where parents are warm and flexible but set few limits on children's behavior. Yet more and more parents are adapting what Diana Baumrind[1] calls authoritative parenting in which limits are stated but parents enforce them with warmth, explanations, and flexibility. Other areas of potential disagreement include the importance you, as parents, want to put on getting straight A's versus doing one's best; the emphasis you want to put on participating versus excelling in sports; and the importance of being popular. Since it is essential to present a consistent approach to your child, you and your partner will need to sort out your differences and decide how you will respond to your child when decisions need to be made. Review your thinking to determine whether your approach is supported by professionals and consistent with the values you support and those supported by the school.

The very activity of you and your spouse coming together to identify your values and expectations can be a rewarding experience. It should unify your purpose and efforts in achieving a successful path for your child. It should reaffirm your family values and confront those aspects of disagreement that could lead to conflict later on. By clarifying your expectations, you can lay down the track on which you want your child to progress.

A Response to *Robert, Mae, and Justin*

Robert and Mae need to discuss and prioritize their goals and values, then transmit a clear message to Justin. If academic success is their highest goal, for example, then the priority should be on achieving excellence in homework.

They should encourage Justin to achieve and remove any doubt that spending after-school time in academic preparation is what he should be doing. In this case, working at the restaurant can be done at other times. The same issue might arise if Justin would want to play community league or CYO basketball or another sport that holds prac-

tices after school. If their priority is the development of personal, social, and athletic skills, then prioritizing these activities would also be appropriate. Showing their support by signing Justin up for the team, arranging for his attendance, and appearing at his games will demonstrate to Justin his parents' support of this activity.

CHAPTER 2

Your Child's Growth and Development

Principle: The middle school years represent a period of enormous physical and emotional growth. Parents need to be aware of these patterns and encourage healthy habits to respond to these dramatic changes.

Ann's Discouragement

Ann was not always happy in the seventh grade: her grades were slipping; her friends were inconsistently loyal; and she felt ugly and fat. She tried to dress differently, trying out styles that deemphasized her thickening figure. Her dad thought this change was funny and stupid and regularly teased her with comments such as, "Here comes Dorky Porky!"

What would you have done?

As a parent, there is nothing more gratifying than to witness the increasing growth and developing capabilities of your child. During the elementary and middle school years, you will see spikes in physical growth: girls generally will achieve 75 percent of their growth by age eight, and boys will achieve the same a year or so later.[1] The changes that occur after that, in the early teen years, are more complex than simply increased height. You will notice your child's increasing command of words, a growing ability to manage emotions, and a developing sense of right and wrong. With this improved self-control your child will develop deeper friendships based on exchanges and helping others rather than on mere proximity. Loyalties will develop. As your child develops more autonomy, she will want to spend more time with friends rather than with you. Expect it. Remember that the ultimate goal is for your child to become self-sufficient.

With your help she should develop manners and display politeness since her peers will shun her if she fails to meet their expected standards. Be sure she can make the transition from your family customs to those of school and the greater society. You will also witness your child's improved hand-eye coordination as she plays ball or a piano, her more skillful small motor coordination as she works on craft projects, and better balance as she rides a bicycle or navigates a skateboard. Strength, ability, and stamina will become apparent.

Your role as a parent during this period of remarkable growth in the middle years is key to your child's successful development. If you can inculcate your basic values at this time, your child will be better prepared for future social changes and temptations. Parents should look to managing the child's environment as much as possible, that is, try to place her in healthy situations in which she learns positive values and experiences success. Do not hesitate to become your child's advocate in this endeavor. As you continue your dialogue with your child, be sure your child knows you are on her side and will come through for her as a trustworthy guide. There is a growing body of evidence that the more nurturing and trustful relationship a child has with her parents, the better she will do in every way.

As a parent it is essential to remember that your child learns a great deal through imitation learning; that is, she will take on the behavior you model for her. Your opportunities to teach good habits by example are great, and if you and your partner have agreed on what values you want to teach, this is an excellent time to convey those messages. Stay connected to your child through regular activities. For example, do not give up watching movies or DVDs with your child. Whereas you once watched Disney fantasies with your young child, now you can watch more mature movies that you can enjoy together and discuss. Pick movies on topics that demonstrate values you want to discuss or that raise issues that are of particular concern to young teens. Ask your child what she thinks about the particular issues the movies present. Teachers at school or the parent-teacher group may have valuable suggestions for appropriate TV programs or movies. These otherwise routine events can become meaningful teaching opportunities as long as you are listening and discussing, not preaching.

One of the dramatic changes you will witness is the onset of puberty. Pediatricians report that middle school children will grow up to two inches and six and a half pounds per year, although growth rates vary widely. We all can recall a classroom where the girls were inches taller than the boys. Girls tend to develop sooner, and you will notice budding breasts in girls as young as eight or nine years old. Menstruation usually begins about two years after the onset of puberty, usually at age twelve to thirteen. Boys enter puberty about a year later, sometime from age nine to fourteen. The peak growth period for boys, like girls, is about two years after the onset of puberty. Changes in boys are noticeable: the cracking voice signals a change in vocal chords; nocturnal emissions or "wet dreams" are normal and something boys cannot control. Boys will experience involuntary erections, some breast enlargement, and one testicle will be lower than the other. All these changes are normal and part of maturity. It should be noted, of course, that growth can be uneven not just among young people, but also in the individual. A girl's feet may grow several sizes before she shoots up in height; a boy's hands may seem to have grown overnight and not fit with the rest of his body. These uneven changes can cause confusion and concern, but are very likely to even out over time.

It is important that such remarkable and confusing changes in your child be met with your support, understanding, and assurance that they are normal. You will need to explain to your child the changes girls and boys undergo during puberty in terms they can understand. If you have discussed sexuality previously with your child, this is another opportunity to build on that knowledge. If you have not ventured into this territory with your child and feel uncertain, consult your pediatrician. Experiences such as a girl's sudden menstrual blood flow, cramping, or the need for vaginal hygiene need not alarm your daughter. Give her assurance that she can participate in normal activities, but be sensitive to her anxieties over issues such as appropriate clothing and modesty. Boys as well will need supportive explanations of how erections, nocturnal emissions, and other hormonal issues fit into their preparation for full adulthood. Your child will welcome your support of increased privacy needs and increasing interest in good grooming. Never tease.

You will also witness changes in temperament during puberty. Your child may react more emotionally, and this is understandable given the dramatic physical and hormonal changes going on within. A concurrent need for orthodontic braces, variation in growth rates among friends, and a burgeoning interest in the opposite sex while maintaining academic expectations all weigh on a young person and easily can push her over the edge. Who among us cannot recall during this period of growth family squabbles over the smallest matters? Parents should remember all that is going on and adopt clear, firm, but supportive guidelines for their children. Yet the need to achieve in school will remain the primary job for young people throughout this dramatic period of change.

Be thoughtful about how you react to your child during this dramatic period. Your child will experience doubts about herself, so it is important to remain encouraging of your child's ability and resilience. It is hoped that your interventions will be a continuation of your previous efforts to build her self-esteem. Look to solidify her confidence and identity by spending time with your child, not just helping with homework—as important as that is. But be aware that your child may think that this activity involves evaluation and may feel stressed. It is helpful for you and your child to become involved in an activity that she enjoys. If it is a sport, practice with her, drive her to practice, and attend her games. Encourage and do not criticize. Leave correction to the coach. It is your job to be on your child's side emotionally, her loyal advocate. If your child enjoys music, facilitate this interest in an instrument or choir. Praise and encourage her efforts, including the truism that practice makes perfect. Whatever your child's choice of activity, this is a period of time when she can expand her world and face new performance and social challenges. You can play a positive role in increasing her competence and confidence. Encourage. Do not criticize. Encourage.

A Response to *Ann's Discouragement*

Parents should realize the child's emotional discomfort and the personal uncertainty in the middle school years. Anticipating these dramatic changes, parents should continue to encourage Ann in everything she does and to assure her of her competence. Often parents will have problem-solving discussions with their children on everything from achieving one's best to being liked by others to attending to physical appearance. Doubts about body image in particular plague middle school girls, so pointing out the normal changes girls go through to become slimmer and more attractive in the high school years can be encouraging. For example, if Ann had an older sister, parents could show her photographs of her sister in junior high school and later in high school. In most cases, the changes are assuring that Ann's discouragement with her body image will be short-lived. And, finally, the dad's teasing is obviously destructive of Ann's self-image and her relationship with her father.

CHAPTER 3

Listening to Your Child

Principle: Effective listening is the key to understanding your child and how to motivate him. Awareness of one's own feelings can help a parent to consider how to express his message.

Tyler's Disobedience

Tyler liked to watch television before school, after school, and in the evenings too. He kept track of every episode of his favorite shows and spent hours in the family room. His parents continued to ask him to clean up the family room, but he neglected the chore. Over time, the family room became quite a mess despite Tyler's parents' reminders. At his wits' end, Tyler's father said, "We give you everything and how do you show your gratitude? You trash the family room and fail to do your chores! When I was your age, I had to keep the yard clean, clean up my room, and make breakfast for the younger kids. All you do is watch TV. You should be ashamed of yourself!"

How would you have handled this situation?

No child is perfect. No parent is perfect. We all have disagreements, misunderstandings, and conflicts. To function as an effective family, we need to communicate effectively, that is, to express loving consideration to one another as we confront different issues. We are resilient, so if we make mistakes, we can rectify them, and we usually rectify them through effective communication. Effective communication is more than sharing information: it requires good listening and the ability to grasp the child's emotional meaning as well as his informational meaning. It is like listening to both the music and the words of a song. If we can grasp the child's feelings as well as his words, we can more fully understand his message, and we are then in a better position to address his problems at school or at home.

Your first job is to become aware of how you sound to your child. Are you communicating in a way *you* would welcome if you were the child? Fathers sometimes joke, "I'm turning into my father!" And mothers echo the feeling. They mean that they can hear the negative patterns of communication they heard from their own parents and are falling into those patterns by learned habit. If those patterns are positive, in terms of support and understanding, by all means retain them. If you experience these patterns as critical and discouraging, however, then you will want to change them. Become conscious of what words you use. What most of us conclude is that we prefer the supportive, understanding communications from our parents, and research bears that out: when children are supported, understood, and encouraged, they tend to do better at school and feel better about themselves. So examine your style of communication. As Schor et al.,[1] note:

> Too often parents choose ineffective, non-accepting ways to communicate with their children. They might give *commands* ("You're going to do as I say, or else!"), *lecture* ("When I was a boy, I had twice as many chores as you!") or *preach* ("You must never behave that way again!") Or they might *criticize* ("You are doing everything wrong today"), *ridicule* ("You looked silly when you struck out"), or *belittle* ("Someone your age should know better.") Be positive and accepting

in the way you talk with your child. Offer praise frequently and be as specific as you can ("You did a wonderful job solving that difficult problem in your math homework tonight.") Let him know how much you appreciate him as he is without his having to struggle to reach your preconceived notions of how you want him to be ("I was so proud just watching you run in the track meet today.")

Surprisingly, your child will be spurred on to do better to please himself and you.

Listening is a skill that you should become conscious of and practice every day. Your good listening tells the child you are interested in what he has to say and that he is important to you. To be an effective listener, try to do the following:

1. Remember that every verbal interaction with your child is your opportunity to influence his character in the direction you and your spouse have agreed upon. So, to the extent you can, focus on what he says without distractions. Give him your undivided attention. For example, if he comes into the room with an urgent look on his face and you are watching a movie at home, put the movie on "pause" and give him your attention.
2. Do not interrupt him. Listen to his entire message even if you have anticipated the situation. If he is telling you about the teacher's unfairness in giving the class an unannounced test, be patient and let him "get it off his chest" before you respond. Use this time to think about your crucial first words.
3. Good listening means being able to summarize what the child has said. With a young child, you

may have to add some information he meant to say, but rephrasing his concern to see if you completely understand it is a good demonstration that you have listened accurately. Especially in complex situations, your ability to summarize in itself helps the child conceptualize the problem and can lead to problem solving more quickly.

4. During your exchange maintain eye contact and display nonverbal acceptance of his message. He will feel he is being received. Nod, for example, to show you are following his presentation.
5. By listening carefully, maintaining eye contact, and giving nonverbal messages, you are receiving his message, and by showing him you have understood his message by being able to summarize his viewpoint, you are showing acceptance of his ideas even when they do not match your own. Don't "jump the gun." This necessary first step sets the stage for your response. Keep in mind this is one of thousands of interactions you will have with your child.
6. Show positive regard by reinforcing the part of the child's statement you agree with. If you disagree with part of his statement, think of how you can phrase your response to encourage the child to see another point of view. Often, asking a question in a supportive way is more effective than a declaration or rejection ("How do you think Charles felt when you pushed into line in front of him at the cafeteria?" might be more effective than "You should not have pushed into line in front of Charles.")
7. Help your child identify and express his feelings in words. This will help him gain control of his emotions and allow him to think before he swings into

action. If you can accomplish this goal, you have given him a great advantage.

Remember that as a parent you are always teaching either by modeling behavior or by your direct statements. With this in mind, you can appreciate that how your child will turn out as an adult will be the accumulation of your messages plus those of other influential people in his life. As his parent you are forming the foundation of his character, and you will want him to learn those values you and your partner identified in chapter 1. How you convey these values, therefore, becomes critically important, for these are tools you use to build his character. This is why we encourage the most constructive methods and discourage methods that can lead your child away from you. The most fruitful situations for parents occur when your messages are conveyed constructively and are consistent with your school and your values. This is where being familiar with the school's mission statement and the curriculum is important. As is often noted, schools with values consistent with your own are built on a belief in the importance of the individual child and the need to respect others, even when we are in disagreement. Echoing these principles in your conversation with your child can go a long way in reinforcing the values he is learning at home and at school.

If we as parents are to be effective communicators, we will need to do a certain amount of self-assessment to identify issues that color our messages. We hope that most of our childhoods were happy and healthy, and if so, we need to recall what contributed to our positive experience. If we experienced conflict, grief, or loss, we need to discern how these unfortunate experiences have affected us. Coming to a clear self-awareness should free us to develop the best family environment for our children, retaining our happiest experiences and ameliorating the negative experiences. We should meld our experiences to develop the most supportive family environment, showing respect, protection, guidance, limit-setting, and conflict resolution. Life moves at a fast pace, so it is easy to overlook this necessary step of self-assessment. But if as a parent you have this awareness, you can more easily supply your own guidance. You will understand more of your own and your child's behavior and will feel more confident in trusting your instincts as you face challenging situations.

Listening empathetically to your child's viewpoint is a fundamental first step in nearly every situation with your child. It allows your child to see that you understand his viewpoint, and that you are on his side for the long run. By repeating this loyalty many times over the years, your child will come to trust you even when you follow your understanding statements with questions that cause him to consider options other than the one he chose. The self-conscious parent is aware of words that come out of his mouth and that his first words in particular will have the most impact on the child. Think of this strategy before you speak and you can develop an approach to respectful problem solving with your child.

There are exceptional situations when even the most sensitive, thoughtful, and self-aware parent will fail in using empathetic understanding. John Gottman[2] uses the term "emotional coaching" for empathetic interventions and warns parents that more than empathy will be needed when:

1. The parent is pressed for time, such as running late in the morning. He suggests setting a later time to discuss the difficulty.
2. Conflict between your child and a sibling (or another child) takes place. He advises discussing the problem with the child alone, not in front of others.
3. You, the parent, are too tired, ill, or upset to do a good job in communicating with your child. Schedule

another time when you are refreshed, because this is hard work.

4. The behavior involves a serious infraction such as the child stealing or committing a crime. The child must see that there are serious consequences, and he should work to develop a healthy conscience.
5. The child is clearly manipulating you simply to get his own way; a skillful negotiation must take place to respect the child's wishes but also to set firm limits.

A Response to *Tyler's Disobedience*

Parents should believe Tyler wants to be a good son and wants to earn the respect and love of his parents. Whenever a child ignores a request from his parents, he is clearly saying his priority is in another place, usually in his personal pursuits. We all are like this sometimes. So the challenge is to examine the entire pattern of rewards parents have been giving Tyler. Have they rewarded him so generously that he has become overconfident and thinks that he need not heed his father? If so, then the parents need to discuss with Tyler what becoming a good family member means (i.e., everyone contributes) and praise him for his efforts in school and with chores. Tyler must come to believe his cooperation will result in a happier family life for his parents and himself. This situation presents an opportunity to build a strong conscience, which is the internalization of family values, in order to be able to decide what is right and wrong.

CHAPTER 4

Collaboration with Your Child's School

Principle: Parents and teachers should form a supportive alliance to benefit the child.

Bradley Fails in Math

Bradley's grades had slipped since a year ago. Now in eighth grade, his parents could not get any explanation from Bradley except that he now hated school and everyone there. He would confine himself to his room for hours at a time and showed little enthusiasm for activities he used to like. His parents could not figure out what was bothering Bradley.

How would you advise Bradley's parents?

Think of all you have invested in your child's life: the time, energy, financial resources, and your commitment that his life will be headed for happiness and success. Parents quickly realize that education is one of the highest priorities along this path and that a good fit between your child and his school is essential. There are many good reasons for choosing a school emphasizing values consistent with those of your family. These schools reflect concern for others, and concern for its children—yours included—and should be congruent with your expectations.

Let's review a little. You have taught your child some basic academic and behavioral skills. At the beginning of school, you made sure that he had all his immunizations, and that a medical doctor cleared him for entry. In choosing a particular school, you have gone through a checklist such as this one:

1. Are the school's expectations clearly stated and do these expectations match your own?
2. Is the learning environment stimulating and appropriate to the needs of your child?
3. Are teacher-student relationships characterized by respect, caring, and an excitement about learning?
4. Does the school encourage and respect cultural differences?
5. Is the principal a good leader and present and welcoming?
6. Do teachers appear to be dedicated, enthusiastic, and skillful in their interactions with their students?
7. Are there sufficient resources to support the full spectrum of learning? Does the school have a library, computer capacity, a music and arts program, physical education and sports opportunities, and a guidance resource?
8. Are they aware of proper nutrition?
9. Is the school and are the students safe?
10. Are the facilities well maintained?
11. Are the costs affordable?
12. Is there a respectful atmosphere that is authentic and respectful of all beliefs?[1]

If your chosen school has met these criteria, you have prepared your child to begin his school year. It is hoped that you have met or are aware of your child's new teacher and soon will become aware of her expectations. Familiarity with the school building and other children in the class is helpful as well (some schools have a buddy system for new students). You are aware of what the child needs to have each day for lunch, physical education, school supplies, and his schedule for the day, including a transportation plan. A child will quickly become aware if his dress is appropriate, so you have checked this out in advance and you have gotten him a backpack or whatever else has been recommended. And, finally, you have prepared the child (and yourself!) emotionally to start the year with optimism and confidence and are ready to review his day with him after school.

If it were just that simple—like plugging in an appliance and letting it run—school would be easy for children. But, of course, it's not. For a child to be successful, he will benefit from continued parental involvement. Yes, you are going to school too, in a manner of speaking. Parents of successful children remain as guides and supporters through the entire process.

Meet your child's teacher and understand her expectations of her students. It is essential for everyone concerned that you form an alliance with the teacher for the mutual benefit of this learning. Be sensitive to the difficulty of her position and respect her boundaries. She is in charge, and you are your child's guide to help him learn and meet these new expectations. If your child later experiences frustrations, you will already have learned the context of his problem. If there are volunteer opportunities to assist the teacher, if you have the time, and if she invites you, you should fit into her system.

Continuing contact with your child's teacher is easier now than it used to be. After an initial face-to-face meeting, a parent can usually communicate via e-mail with the teacher if there is an issue for discussion. Periodically, there will be parent-teacher conferences, an opportunity to spend fifteen or twenty minutes with the teacher to examine your child's progress in various subjects of study, and to evaluate your child's social behavior with the other children and the school. Do not miss this opportunity to meet. Bring your questions about your child's performance to the meeting and have your questions answered. Do not worry about how the child's behavior reflects on you; instead, focus on the educational challenges for the child. After all, it is an educational process, and every student can improve in some way. You and the teacher are allies in helping your child advance.

Here are some typical questions parents ask the teacher after discussing the school experience with their spouse and child:

1. How well is my child doing in each subject area? What are his strengths and weaknesses and how were these evaluated?
2. What should we as parents be doing at home to support his best school performance?
3. How does my child interact with classmates? Does he appear to have friends? Are there situations where he displays or lacks confidence or has responded to social difficulty?
4. Is there any area, academic or social, where he might need or benefit from a special assessment?
5. Has he attended classes regularly and been on time?
6. Has his homework been satisfactory and has it been turned in on time? Does he understand the concepts being taught by his participation in classroom discussions?
7. Do you feel your child is being encouraged? Does he appear to be happy?

Be sure you get your questions answered, and leave with a plan for improvement with next steps on which you and the teacher agree. If he has homework, understand your role in assisting your child with it and, at a minimum, check his work with him at home before he goes on to other activities. Experienced parents all agree that a lot of learning takes place at home. Or, to put it another way, successful students have parents who review their children's work every day.

At times problems will arise, and while most parents do not like to hear of problems, it is best to think of them as learning opportunities. Find out the specifics of the problem, whether it is academic, such as a failure on a test, or behavioral, such as an argument with a classmate. First, discuss the issue calmly and completely with your child. Meet with the teacher in person and collaboratively try to find the needed correction. Sometimes the right course cannot be decided in a single meeting, but since you as parents know your child best, you should be able to propose a correction to the child's behavior. Involve the child in your deliberations and help him understand that many children experience such difficulties, and that the most important part is correcting them then and there. Encourage his corrective efforts. For example, if the child has been failing to hand in his homework for a week, the parent should discuss the problem with the child, meet with the teacher, and agree on a course of action. That course might be establishing a schedule after school with no TV or video games until homework is finished. A parent should then review the homework and, if problems are detected, correct them immediately using as encouraging an approach as possible. Most of these problems are solved with closer and supportive parental supervision.

Problems that have arisen in the past include those with classmates, with school subjects, and with school rules. The most common social problem is some kind of rejection the child experiences. For example, a friend may not want to spend time with your child for a while. Discuss the situation carefully with your child and try to extend support and encouragement. Ask the child if he has any ideas of how to address the problem. Sometimes you may involve the teacher, and at other times you may work to get your child to understand how each person in the group feels and what he might do differently. Making new friends is always an option. Frequently, rejections are fleeting, and individuals rejoin their groups in a few days. If the problem persists through the school year, and your efforts have not changed the situation, a psychologist or mental health therapist may be consulted.

Academic problems, or problems with a school subject, require close consultation with the teacher to identify where the child is experiencing difficulty. At times there may be miscommunication between teacher and student. At other times, the student is challenged to think in a new way about a topic. At still other times, you may discover your child seems unable to learn the skill no matter what you try. Teachers are usually good about providing extra help either before or after school. If you yourself are experienced in a particular subject, like mathematics, you can provide additional help. Or you may look for a tutor. If these strategies fail, perhaps further diagnostic assessment by a school psychologist is needed.

The third category of common problems involves conflicts over following school rules. Know the student handbook published by your school as well as the teacher's classroom rules, and be sure your student follows these rules. Failure to follow the rules will result in some form of discipline, but remember that school discipline is another form of teaching. School discipline should show respect for the child and take into account the child's background and capabilities, as well as his efforts to improve the situation. A child should never be humiliated or physically punished at school. In your home you should demonstrate respect for the school processes and be a positive model of cooperation. Do not be hesitant about supplying lots of reminders, because few children (or adults) get everything right the first time. In the rare case where you sense an enduring personality conflict between your child and his teacher, you can ask for a consultation with the principal if your interventions with the teacher have failed to resolve the situation. These cooperative consultations are directed toward what is educationally best for your child.

A final word about homework: parents can help their child develop good homework habits that will serve him well throughout his educational career if they train him early on to work carefully, thoughtfully, and persistently. This is best accomplished by reviewing your child's work daily until he can do it on his own.

A Response to *Bradley Fails in Math*

First, Bradley's withdrawal is a serious concern. Parents should continue to patiently discuss events with Bradley until Bradley comes to a point where he reveals the nature of his disappointment. Since this can take time, parents should not give up. They should continue with their normal activities with Bradley until the vulnerable moment of self-revelation occurs. It can be during a ride to the grocery store or a bedtime discussion. Bradley will eventually share his pain if his parents display enough patience and understanding for him to trust them with his problem. He has to believe they will be on his side. In this case, Bradley feels humiliated because he is failing math, his first failure in school. Extremely self-critical, he is punishing himself by withdrawing from other activities he likes. He is embarrassed to ask for help. Bradley's parents learn where the problem has occurred: it's prealgebra and they do not feel competent to tutor him. With Bradley's acknowledgement, they call his teacher and arrange for a meeting with the four of them. With the parents giving support to Bradley, they go over the problem areas and then arrange some before-school special help from the teacher. She assures Bradley he can recover his old level of proficiency. This meeting fractures the emotional logjam and Bradley's efforts are restored. The problem vanishes shortly thereafter.

CHAPTER 5

A Note about Girls

Principle: Parents would be wise to become familiar with the unique problems girls face as they try to succeed socially and academically. Parents should engage their daughters sensitively in thought-provoking discussions to keep them on the right path for success.

Jennifer's Sudden New Interests

Jennifer has been a stellar student since she began school. She has earned A's in every subject and scored in the 90th percentile on national tests. In the sixth grade, she won a school award for being one of their highest achievers. Now in the eighth grade, Jen tells you she doesn't want to do homework. She would rather hang out at the mall and go to the weekly dances at the local high school with her friend. Boys seem to be calling every night for her.

What do you do?

Let's begin with the obvious: while many of the child-raising principles apply to both girls and boys, there are unique differences between our daughters and sons. To become a better prepared parent, we should consider these characteristics and factor them into our parenting plans.

We have made the point that parenting is teaching the values, skills, and behaviors we believe will result in a happy and successful life for our child. We have emphasized the importance of couples determining what their personal values are and how best to teach them. In this section we will refer to those principles that support the development of competent and confident girls and reinforce the stance parents should maintain throughout the difficult middle years.

Most parents agree that raising daughters becomes more complex as they emerge from elementary school and move on to middle school and junior high. Dramatic changes begin to take place before parents' eyes: girls become more physically mature and begin to resemble young women; girls seek independence from parental authority and move closer to their peer groups; and girls face new intellectual challenges and make some accommodation to social pressures while continuing to achieve. These are big changes.

In the middle years a girl's physical development contributes to many feelings of discomfort. Budding breasts, pubic hair, and beginning menstruation with its accompanying pain and discomfort are the most dramatic changes. Her body begins to transform from compact and straight to a shapelier face, breasts, and hips. Hormonal changes produce emotional reactions with more frequent upsets and tearfulness. A girl becomes more concerned with her appearance, clothes and, predictably, boys. She is growing up in a media blitz that promotes images of costly material goods, clothes and make-up, and exaggerated romantic relationships. These ads imply that she should be moving into this zone of experimentation right away. Yet she is likely to see herself as far less beautiful than the thin and glamorous teen models in these ads. In fact, she may feel fat, mistaking the body's normal developmental thickening for signs of being out-of-shape. She may alter her eating habits in unhealthy ways through cutting back her food intake or by avoiding certain foods. Confused about where her body fits into fashion, she may want loose-fitting clothes that conceal or, at the other extreme, she may choose clingy and revealing outfits intended for more sophisticated figures. On the other hand, while your daughter may be appearing older by the month, she may not have mastered basic hygiene quite yet (for instance, not showering daily). This will come in time as she observes her peers and hears your gentle reminders.

At the same time, she will be growing in independence. In elementary school, girls often attach to small groups of friends that remain relatively constant. In this new phase of middle school, she will likely move to a tighter clique of friends who expect a certain conformity. At age ten or so she might develop a best friend in whom she confides. She will explore life's new social demands in pairs or in her clique, and you as parents may be moved to an ancillary role and may, in some cases, generally be regarded as clueless. Don't be offended. (More on this later.)

Girls will depend on one another to interpret their social context, particularly in their efforts to be accepted, able, and attractive. They will track and experiment with interest from boys. It is the unusual girl who is confident about herself, her place in this context, and her attractiveness to others. She will more likely want the social approval of her group and conform to its unique norms. The girl who departs from these norms risks the characteristic form of girls' aggression: exclusion. For example, a girl may find herself not invited to a party or sleep-over for some seemingly random reason such as achieving at a higher level than others. In her book *Odd Girl Out*, Rachel Simmons[1] documents how girls display their aggression against one another through gossip and exclusion, and how they exert pressure to conform to the group's expectations. This occurrence is not atypical for middle school girls, and parents can play a significant role in helping their daughter cope with these sorts of social "bumps in the road." Being aware of when your daughter may be the subject of exclusion and normalizing this experience as one that most women have gone through in middle school can help. Equally important, parents can help reduce feelings of social rejection by encouraging a wide variety of friends and activities. Having more than one group of friends or more than one activity can act as "self-esteem insurance," such that when one area is not going as well, your daughter can turn to other people and activities to feel good about herself. It is hoped that these strategies will reduce a girl's vulnerability to rejection, even for the short duration it occurs.

All the while these changes are taking place, a girl is still expected to achieve intellectually. Most girls advance in language arts in the elementary grades but, beginning in middle school when application of skills is required, the challenges increase. Even more crucial, there appears to be a crisis point for many girls in the junior high years. Girls who were high achievers in their early years come to believe that if they assert their intelligence, they will not be liked or accepted and relent in their efforts to achieve. These girls pick up signals that to be liked means being submissive, noncompetitive, and "nice." Some girls avoid taking the most challenging academic subjects. Carol Gilligan[2] points to what she calls "the tyranny of niceness" in which girls compromise their initiative and ambition in order to be socially approved. There are numerous messages in our culture that idealize a girl as the helper, the nurturer, or the pleaser and not as an achiever. Girls must confront this message, too, in determining what emphasis they will place on academic and social opportunities. Parents need to be alert to their daughter's thinking on these issues and continue to support her achievement efforts in these critical years.

So what are parents to do on a day-to-day basis amid all the turbulence in their daughter's life? First, it is helpful to become knowledgeable of the changes the girl is experiencing and to continue to listen supportively to whatever problem she presents. As increasing independence would imply, a parent must be sensitive and patient about giving direct suggestions. By now your daughter knows where you stand on most issues, so direct instruction should be supplied when she is truly open to suggestion. At times, however, an independent girl is less than totally open to suggestions, and a more indirect approach is more successful. Effective teaching involves asking questions that can lead her to conclusions she can discover and claim for herself. For example, if your twelve-year-old daughter wants to wear a revealing blouse to the school dance, you can ask her how she will be received not only by the boys but by her girl friends and the teachers attending the dance. Most girls at this age will choose not to wear a provocative outfit (unless their friends also do so) but are more likely to wear one in response to an argument with a parent.

Experienced parents have said that their treatment of their daughters differs from their treatment of their sons because of their desire to protect. Protect from what? Most protective feelings involve sexual vulnerability and the parents' anxiety that their daughter might be exploited. We know that locking up our daughters in the proverbial Rapunzel's tower will likely backfire in a burst of preadolescent rebellion. What parents should keep in mind is that the task is to educate the girl to become aware of the hazards of being female in our contemporary and at times predatory society. It is likely she has grown up amid reports of violence, rape, and sexual exploitation. It is in the news every day. It is important for parents to use these current news events as opportunities to discuss good decision-making and staying safe, and to distinguish between romantic notions and realistic behavior. It is hoped that these conversations will be extensions of those you have been having for years about how to evaluate situations.

Fathers, more than mothers, report feeling anxious and controlling of their daughters. While a certain amount of preventive anxiety can be useful, it is important to remember that parents want to teach their daughters to eventually be in control of their own lives. This means the challenge is to teach daughters to evaluate social situations involving boys or men based on parental insights and experience so that they can be well skilled in making good judgments when parents are no longer present. This teaching of self-care in the middle years includes gradually exposing the girl to limited social opportunities with built-in controls (the school dance with chaperones versus the Rave without adults present). The teaching is a continuous process aimed at social competence. Remember how you taught her to ride a bicycle. You began by providing maximum support and safety and, as she demonstrated her ability to take care of herself, you loosened your control, sometimes shadowing her. Over time she learned how to handle herself, and you could then stand back and admire her agility.

Fathers are their daughters' first exposure to men, and the model fathers have presented constitutes the basis of the girl's learning about how men behave. JoAnn Deak[3] cites a girl who gives a good description of what a father should be:

> The ideal father…is understanding, with a sense of humor, around when you need him, but not too nosy, a shoulder to cry on, openly loves my mom, a good role model, and always pushes you to do your best, not too hard, lets you be your own person, and loves you for who you are, unconditionally. What I love most about my father is that I know that he'll love me forever, no matter what, and I love his hilarious sense of humor. If I could change one thing, it would be that he'd be around more often. Other than that, he understands what I want him to, and other girl stuff wasn't really meant for a dad to understand.

This excerpt is instructive in that it lists the father's understanding and support of his daughter, his encouragement, his sensitivity in how hard to push, and his sense of humor to balance the message. His modeled love for his wife and unconditional love for his daughter transcend all problems. After all, these are the most effective teaching conditions to build a girl's strong interior self, which can then confront social and academic challenges successfully and, as a result, build confidence and resilience.

Like a good poker player, a parent has to know when to play a card and when to hold onto one. In other words, there will be times when your increasingly independent daughter will reject you. She may no longer want to participate in some family activities you once enjoyed; she may call you clueless and ask you not to attend her sports activities; or she may want you far, far away from her interactions with boys. Even more dramatic, she may say the words nearly every parent has heard at one time or another: "Get out of my life!" Expect this shift in her attitude, but remember it is not about you. Do not take these harsh words literally. Never retaliate out of injured feelings. If you have done a good job as a parent, the ringing of her own words followed by your silence will excite a sense of guilt in her so that any comment from you will not be necessary. Remain calm and choose a later time when rational communication can take place. In the meantime, think of the questions you need to ask your daughter to address the source of her frustrations and help her clarify her feelings. Remember, she is going through a turbulent time. Is there anyone who would ever want to go through junior high school again?

Follow your intuition with your daughter. She is swimming in a whirlpool of conspicuous consumption, messages of premature sexual involvement, excessive competition, experimental drug and alcohol use, unhealthy nutrition, all while trying to meet parental expectations in school. She will need your patient support and your model of unshakeable love.

She will also need loyal friends and, in this regard, research shows that parental involvement in activities such as team sports, music, or other endeavors correlates with a sense of social competence. In these activities as well as in other school challenges, teach resilience to your daughter. Keep going. Face the social and academic challenges and learn to solve problems in all situations. Do not avoid them and do not give up.

A Response to *Jennifer's Sudden New Interests*

As we have discussed previously, parents should maintain a continuous dialogue with their child so that dramatic changes like this do not occur. Continuous dialogue gives parents the opportunity to keep their child on track in terms of priorities they share. But if parents encounter this sudden interest in socialization, it is time for a problem-solving conference. A good academic and a good social life need not be incompatible if the agreement is, "work before play," and competent work at that. One parent in our group recalled that his daughter was receiving a plethora of telephone calls at night until mom said, "Get all your work done first, let me look it over, and then *you can make and receive phone calls for two hours." (Parents may have to "hold" a cell phone during study time to assure this agreement is kept.) This compromise was part of a larger discussion of achieving success academically and socially. The mom said she did not and probably could not restrict every social instinct the girl had, but she could begin to educate her about the costs and benefits of her decisions. The mother also checked out Jennifer's friends to be sure their values were complementary to her own. The mom joked that this period with Jennifer was like a toboggan ride for about two years, but Jennifer maintained her grades, attended weekend social functions, and excelled in sports, too. Jennifer was happy with the way things turned out.*

CHAPTER 6

A Note about Boys

Principle: Parents should become familiar with the boy's struggle to believe in himself as a young man and should be sure to teach him alternative ways to feel confident and competent.

Cut from the Team

Your son Patrick has played basketball in CYO and community teams from an early age. He follows the local high school and college teams and roots for his NBA favorite. He tries out for the seventh-grade select club team, which everyone knows is the stepping stone to the high school varsity team, but he is cut and will have no chance to make the team. He is devastated and wants to give up on sports, perhaps on everything.

What do you say?

I have a colleague who is a fraternal twin. He tells the story that upon their birth an uncle visited them in the hospital and pinned a ten-dollar bill on his sister's pink sweater and a hundred-dollar bill on his blue sweater. Thus we have it from birth: a signal that boys will be treated differently from girls. I believe cultural attitudes have moved closer to equality in the contemporary United States, but there remain many inequalities in attitude, if not in fact. Why mention this cultural favoritism in this section on boys rather than on girls? Because with this favoritism come higher expectations, and boys feel it from an early age.

The expectation is that a boy will lead, dominate, and be strong and reasonable. If he is not, he can be regarded as weak, irrelevant, and at times, a "sissy." A boy senses this from early on and, when placed in a school setting, he feels some inchoate tension. Parents can help him considerably by being aware of these cultural expectations and tensions and by placing him in carefully considered environments. As we have discovered, helping the child understand, consider, and express his tensions will more likely result in a good adjustment for the child.

We know that boys generally adjust more slowly than girls to the school setting in the early years. Boys are generally more physically exuberant and impulsive; they are slower than girls to grasp language arts and reading in the early years; teachers tend to express more criticism as well as praise toward boys. It is also well known that behavioral problems in school tend to be attributed to boys and, even further, problems with the law, including juvenile court cases, tend disproportionately to involve boys.[1] So it is important for parents to see to it that a boy's adjustment to school is as smooth as possible. Early patterns of adjustment can have long-lasting implications for the boy's development.

Why are boys more apt to get into trouble than girls? You can see it in their play where they assume more active, sometimes heroic, roles. They are more assertive, outspoken, and competitive. They tend to choose games involving physical expression nearly always with other boys; they play by the rules to win and are less concerned about the feelings of others in their games. There is less discussion of feelings and empathy except for one emotion: anger. Parents too often pass off these cultural traits with the aphorism "Boys will be boys" and fail to explore the emotions involved.

The emotional life of boys is seriously underarticulated, and this is an area where parents can help. The challenge for a boy is to grow up to be a good man, but the definition of manhood is seldom spelled out. If we rely on the popular media, the boy will fall prey to some unfortunate sexual stereotypes. Instead, parents should consider what kind of man they want him to be.

To be valued as a competent and successful man requires strength of character. When we think of the ideal young man, we can see there are a number of ways to achieve success. He can be physically strong, of course. Men get respect for this. He can be athletically skilled; we have an entire section of the newspaper devoted to men who excel in this area. He can accumulate wealth and with it exert influence. Or he can display diligence and intelligence and succeed by contributing his special abilities. He can be regarded as physically handsome or possess a unique talent such as musical ability. Or he can achieve a level of social skill or moral authority where people trust his judgment. All these avenues invite a boy to gain dominance, control, or strength in some competitive arena that can satisfy the challenge of becoming a man. Few boys can see these multiple paths to success, and many experience frustrations in following a path that does not work well for them. As parents, we can help boys see that there are many paths up the mountain. One example is the junior high school boy who loved basketball but was cut in tryouts for the school team. He went on to become involved in drama and succeeded in this area, earning the esteem of his peers.

Part of a boy's confusion is due to the poor job our culture does in providing messages to boys about what they will need to achieve maturity. Parents can provide this essential confirmation. If parenting involves teaching children to integrate the rules of society within their own minds, then one essential goal of parenting is to help the child develop a good conscience. As he becomes older, a boy should become more thoughtful about deciding what is right and what is wrong for him. He should be applying these lessons taught by his parents and teachers to the world he encounters and be encouraged to live out these lessons.

Books on parenting these days rightfully emphasize emotional intelligence, emotional literacy, or accurate empathy.[2] Whichever term you use, it invites parents to help their children, particularly their sons, to identify, consider, articulate, and act upon thought-out feelings. It is a building process that, if practiced during the boy's developing years, can lead to social success and minimize social problems at school, in sports, and in relationships.

Parents should model the successful behavior they are trying to teach. The effects of modeling are enormous and can lead the child in the right direction. Maintaining a dialogue with your child as he grows up is important as well because the alert parent will seize the many opportunities to instruct and encourage. One parent I know says he has always given his children "commercials" about what leads to a successful life. He has regularly encouraged attending college, treating friends (of both sexes) well, and maintaining integrity in dealings with others. It is not surprising his children have been successful and well adjusted.

In day-to-day interactions with boys, parents will find them testing the rules, experimenting with new behavior, and questioning parental judgment. Remember, parenting is teaching, and if you as a parent respond with impatience or punitive tactics, you are forfeiting your opportunity to teach successful adjustment. A wise parent can absorb his child's excesses, even insults, and turn them around to teach the child why he is misguided in his thinking. Parenting is a job that requires alertness, patience, and thoughtfulness.

A parent who understands this concept can be phenomenally successful. The parent will understand that his son will be testing rules as he grows older. The parent provides a healthy model for the child to emulate, and if the child experiences some difficulty, the parent is alert to the teaching opportunity. He is ready to absorb the exuberant excess, whether it is misbehavior, name calling, or disrespect. He patiently maintains a dialogue and with respectful questioning brings the child around to see why his misbehavior will not result in social success. A common example is the young son's refusal to do his assigned chore of cleaning up the family room because his younger sister does not do that job. The parent's challenge is to get him to see how every member of the family contributes according to his or her ability and that these tasks change with growth. He will be appreciated for his contributions and will be regarded as a good son if he does his part. This response is intended to get the boy to see the larger picture, to understand his contribution, and to feel rewarded for being a good son. Children usually want to please their parents and eventually comply.

Of course, we make occasional mistakes. We criticize, demean, or even become physically coercive. I believe it was Mark Twain who said that violence is the product of an exhausted mind.[3] To raise morally competent and successful children, we should be careful not to become so overly impatient or over-stressed. There is much research to support the warning that harsh discipline such as spanking, verbal intimidation, threats, or humiliation are counterproductive, producing only superficial compliance but camouflaging the resulting resentment and diminished self-confidence.[4] Over time, it produces a sense of helplessness, confusion, and anger most often related to social problems and violence. Even worse, harsh discipline suppresses the boy's ability to think through the problem and utilize his internal controls.

Mothers can provide a boy's emotionally secure base from which to explore the world. It is essential the boy feels that his mother is on his side, that he can have just enough emotional support, which he will need as he develops more and more independence. If she is too casual or neglectful in this area, the boy risks feeling insecure and anxious. If she is overprotective or controlling, he could become discouraged in seeking independence and being adventuresome. What is even more problematic is that he could feel stressed at her overinvolvement, and this could interfere with the development of his gender identity. The challenge is to evaluate how much support the boy needs and to provide him with that right amount.

Fathers provide the model of manhood for the boy. I recall a poster long ago of a boy hand-in-hand with his dad walking through the woods. The caption was "Take time." What could be more important than taking time with your son? There is considerable research to show that fathers who are emotionally involved in their child's life produce children who are academically successful and socially well adjusted.[5] Many fathers volunteer to coach a team or mentor an activity. In the best of circumstances, a boy can learn sportsmanship, which encompasses behavior involved in winning as well as behavior involved in losing. Activities can teach teamwork and how to follow the rules. If the coach or mentor is consistent with the values you are teaching your son, it can add to his successful moral development.

If parents fail to guide, a boy is left to explore these complex emotions among his equally confused peers. Middle school and junior high school leading into adolescence make for a turbulent sea. Boys have not yet developed their self-confidence, and comparisons are inevitable. Even an apparently successful boy feels apprehensive about making social errors lest he be rejected by his peers. What he says, what he wears, what he does are all critiqued by his potentially judgmental peer group, few of whom know for sure what constitutes the right path. The early teenage years are exploratory and insecure for a boy until he reaches a time when he becomes more certain of himself and his values, and he is less guided by peer judgments. I recall many years ago in high school that before a football game, a boy on the sidelines sang the national anthem solo when everyone else was too self-conscious to try. I admired his courage to display his talent, to stand out, to risk potential peer rejection. We all hope to feel that confidence.

Parents who become aware of the unique tensions within their sons and have prepared themselves to guide them through good modeling, skillful intervention, and development of a strong conscience, will be most likely to see their sons emerge into confident and successful young men.

A Response to *Cut from the Team*

Despite our best efforts, we do not always succeed in every activity. But even with such a bitter disappointment as being cut from the team, there are often opportunities through which a boy can find success. At first the parent should respond to the sense of loss; it is grieving. In time, however, new opportunities should emerge that can substitute for the old. A boy who is wedded to the sports model should come to see other models of success—other special abilities that can define him and lead to achievement. As with all parent-child discussions, parents should utilize and model articulation of feelings, especially empathy and problem solving. Guiding the young man to a new path, one he chooses for himself and can count on his parents for support with, will constitute a vital life lesson. This redefinition will take place over time; it should be viewed as a continuing process that will take place over a year or two. Supportive and understanding parents can supply the necessary steps to form their son's ladder of success.

CHAPTER 7

The Harmonious Family: Siblings without Rivalry

Principle: Parents should convey the idea that sufficient love and attention are available for each child. Competition means to do one's personal best and support other family members' best efforts as well. As a family, you are all in life's struggles together.

Emily's Jealousy

Ed and Susan have three children: Richard, fourteen; Emily, twelve; and Deborah, six. Richard is completing his science project based on a collection of igneous and metamorphic rocks showing changes in the earth's conditions. His teacher has said he has earned an A for the project, and he would like to sponsor the project at the state science fair. One day Richard finds Emily painting his rock collection with her red nail polish. Richard is furious.

What do you do?

Even the most loving and harmonious family will experience conflict between siblings. It is easily understandable because every child wants his parents' love and attention, and a child will witness occasions when parents' attention is given to another. It is clear that to succeed socially in our world, we all need to learn to share attention and affection. Others have emotional needs as important as our own. This sharing becomes an important lesson parents are called upon to teach, and if done successfully, it can produce a happy family where children support one another while they strive for their own achievement.

How can parents accomplish this? First, parents must appreciate the differences among their children. While there may be genetic similarities among brothers and sisters, there will also be differences. Parents should appreciate these differences and support each child's unique strengths. Be conscious about not favoring one child over another. Be aware of your own prejudices and try to treat each child fairly. If your children feel you are fair minded in treating them, there will be less reason for conflict. Fairness, of course, may not mean equal treatment. The very fact that one child is older than another introduces different capabilities. Your fair treatment should be appropriate for the age of the child and take into account other conditions such as disabilities.[1]

Children learn to be competitive as part of their adaptation to our society. Parents should encourage competition against oneself rather than against other siblings. An analogy would be a distance runner trying for his personal best time in his event, a mile race for example. He is competing against himself more than against others. If others run the mile well, then they deserve congratulations; but he makes his own best effort. This emotional frame of mind allows for supporting others such as siblings, and in a family where parents display a generous love, they learn that there is enough love and attention for everyone. Parental love is not a zero sum game. If parents adopt adversarial thinking, siblings will experience tensions with one another. To counter this, parents can teach their children the healthier pattern of self-referenced competition.

Another aspect of sibling rivalry that can undermine family harmony is the child's perception that his universe is his family. Actually, his family, including siblings, should be his source of support. Parents can explain this benefit and help him contend with the competitive forces outside the family. The middle school years in particular can be an ideal time for a child to try his hardest in school, adjust to the realistic outcomes of his efforts, and experience the support of his family.

As we have said in previous sections, good parenting means continuous guidance. As children mature and gain independence, they will challenge you as well as antagonize their siblings. Good parenting means being as prepared as possible for these emotional growth spurts, and this preparation most often includes maintaining the principles of support put forth in this book. In other words, just setting forth the goals of mutual support among siblings will not be enough. Parents will have to monitor interactions between siblings and remind them of the principles being taught. It will be a continuing process.

Because of the demands of school and parental expectations, children will at times become upset. The supportive listening and encouragement previously described will continue to be necessary. Encourage children to admit their mistakes and have them experience you as the parent ready to help them correct the situation. Discourage tattling; rather, try to build a good conscience in each child so that he will internalize the rule and guide his behavior accordingly.

As children experience a dramatic change in their lives, they may act out in some way calling for attention. A typical example is the birth of a brother or sister. In order for the child not to feel displaced or experience a loss of attention, experienced parents make special efforts to prepare the child for this new addition and find a special role for the child. A big brother or big sister can share in the attention, which at times can be ongoing when it involves grandparents, friends, and extended family. To maintain healthy sibling relationships, the child must witness sufficient love and attention for each child. An informative example of this situation is the grandmother who had paid extensive attention to her first grandchild, Gloria. When Gloria was four years old, her parents had a little boy, and grandmother, loving babies, threw her total attention to the baby. Feeling ignored, Gloria innocently asked her father, "Doesn't grandma love me anymore?" Of course everyone loved Gloria, but with the excitement of a new baby, her grandmother and parents lost sight of the fact that Gloria felt displaced. Unless corrected, it could initiate a deep and lasting sense of sibling rivalry.

A similar misstep can occur in the sensitive situation of marriage when siblings from different families try to blend together. Parents must be particularly self-aware and careful to be supportive and fair to all the children lest they feel favoritism and a loss of support. Stories of cruel stepmothers and stepfathers abound in literature, and children are familiar with them. Parents should talk through these concerns with each child, assure each child he is valued, and back up that expressed assurance by honoring each child's personal space, belongings, and privacy. To do otherwise invites sibling tension.

There is some debate about how siblings should address their squabbles. Parental interventions can run the gamut from intervening directly and suggesting solutions to the problem, to the complete opposite—allowing the children to work their problems out for themselves. Parents must interpret the capabilities of their children. Some may need more guidance than others. More mature children may only need parents as guideposts. But since there is usually an age difference between squabbling siblings, parents should always monitor the difficulty and have the final say so that their conclusion is consistent with the values being taught, not the least of which is fairness. Most parents have good judgment about these matters if they thoroughly understand the situation.

Finally, family harmony can be facilitated with weekly family meetings or some family forum that parents establish for everyone to have their say. Although a family is not a true democracy, everyone's concern is legitimate, creating a challenge for parents to find an appropriate response that meets the complaint. If parents are aware of children's concerns on a day-to-day basis, there is seldom an emergency because parents are already working on the problems they have seen. Family meetings can demonstrate that there is enough parental love for everyone, and everyone can work together for success.

A Response to *Emily's Jealousy*

We would like to think each of our children is getting enough personal support, attention, and recognition to feel confident and successful. We would also like to feel that as they gain confidence, each child will not feel jealous of, or in competition with, a sibling, but rather be supportive of her sibling's success. In this case, Emily has not achieved this and requires a review of where she may have gone off track. Such an act on Emily's part may reflect a temporary regression or a larger, long-standing issue of deprivation. Parents not only must try to get Emily to experience success for herself, but also to model appreciation of her brother's success to others in the family in the interest of harmony. This will take some sensitive listening to Emily's point of view and some additional efforts by Emily to succeed in areas she prefers. Having family meetings during which everyone's viewpoint is supported may also contribute to a climate of mutual support.

CHAPTER 8

Discipline as Teaching

Principle: Disciplinary opportunities provide teachable moments in which parents can supportively reinforce those values they have defined as leading to success.

Jimmy Eats the Snacks

Jimmy comes home after school and eats all the cookies and sweet snacks his mother has put aside for school lunches for himself and his two brothers. Dad discovers Jimmy's disobedience and spanks him. Dad says he will not tolerate Jimmy stealing food and tells him next time he'll get a real beating. Jimmy, in shame and pain, skulks off to his room.

What do you think Jimmy has learned?

Probably the closest synonym to parenting is guidance. As parents we are responsible for guiding our children onto a track that will lead to happiness, personal success, and social capability. Ideally, we should be present all the time to be assured the child is learning what we believe to be the correct principles. But that would be a futile chore and, in fact, we hope the child will learn all this socially correct behavior, integrate it, and be able to apply it on his own. The role of the parent, then, is to teach children well from direct instruction, modeling the desired behaviors, and identifying others who will convey those values consistently. We have already described some beginning points: identifying family values, utilizing best parenting practices to teach these values, becoming patient and self-aware listeners, and finally, managing the child's environment as best we can to achieve these goals of child development.

It is not an impossible task. Children want their parents' approval, and when we convey positive attention and approval for the behavior and values we express, our children will want to adopt these behaviors. Most parents recognize the extent children will go to earn their parents' attention. They will even misbehave to get it. So the challenge of good guidance is to deliver our approval whenever the child behaves in ways we have set out for him. We hope this praise will be frequent. Psychologists like to say, "Catch the child being good."

As the child gets older, the application of approval to desirable behaviors gets more complex. As parents, we must be alert to the myriad of new demands the child will face at school: new rules in the classroom, new children to play with, new teachers' expectations, their own physiological changes and, possibly, changing situations at home (e.g., new jobs, a move, a death or birth in the family). We should expect our children to make some mistakes, no matter how well we have prepared them. The alert parent is continually listening to his child, and when problems arise, the parent is ready to teach the child a problem-solving response. Some common problems are the refusal to comply with school requirements, avoidance of responsibilities, sibling rivalry, difficulty completing homework or chores, controlling impulses, and poor choices of friends. If a parent is careful about managing his own tensions and has continued to maintain a healthy relationship with his spouse, then he should be able to devote full attention to the task of teaching.

We realize children's development is continuous, but sometimes they seem to grow up quickly, right before our eyes. We find our young school-age children developing independence and wanting to spend more time with friends rather than with us. Some parents find this transition hard to accept because there is a wish for our children to remain young, but we must encourage this growth to further prepare them for increasingly complex social situations. Children should have opportunities to try out their learned behavior in new settings. What parent has not been pleased when other parents comment that your child has played well and been polite with their own child? In other words, your child has been able to apply his social skills successfully in a new situation.

The best disciplinary approach for the parent is helping his child relearn. To correct an error means, first, to analyze the situation by asking what barrier the child has run into that failed to produce the desired choice. Was the expectation clear? Did the child understand what steps were needed? Did the parent or teacher clearly encourage the child's efforts? Was there consistency of message between teacher and parents? This identification of where the breakdown occurred will guide the parent to the next step: a supportive intervention.

Most contemporary parents utilize behavioral methods to teach the child discipline. We have mentioned the use of encouragement, positive attention, and praise following the child's good behavior. This is most important and too often neglected. Positive, rewarding comments given regularly will encourage the child to repeat the good behavior and build a reservoir of self-esteem that will serve him well when his confidence is shaken by a mistake. When a child misbehaves, parents typically utilize a "time-out." A time-out means removing the child from the positive and stimulating activity in the child's environment. He loses the opportunity for praise and positive attention, but can regain it if, after a short period of reflection, he corrects his behavior.

Parents sometimes think of these two methods in automotive terms: they use the accelerator, or positive rewarding, to encourage the child to repeat the positive behavior, such as doing his homework. They use a time-out as the brake to terminate the misbehavior by loss of privileges, which can then be regained by correcting the behavior.

These somewhat simple tools require parents to observe and listen closely to their children because behavior change comes with consistency of application. Taking the situation one step further, such as teaching the child a desirable pattern of behavior, some parents utilize a token economy of reward. They use a token system based on the principle we have described: rewarding the child's behavior to increase it in frequency and consistency. A typical example would be the parent's wish to teach the middle school child to clean up his room each day. There are several steps to consider in setting up such a system.

1. Define the target behavior and communicate it to the child. For example, the target is to have the child pick up all toys, clothes, and materials from his floor, bed, and chairs and hang them up and/or put them away at a mutually agreed-upon time of the day.
2. Be sure you and the child agree on what a cleaned up room means.
3. Identify a short-term and immediate reward that motivates the child to do these things. Age-appropriateness of the reward is essential. For example, money seldom motivates a younger child. Parental praise is always paired with the reward and later, when the short-term reward is removed, the praise continues.
4. In a place where the child can see it, put up a chart that displays the days of the week and has a place

for a gold star or symbol to signify successful performance. Be generous in supplying stars and small rewards at the start so the child will want to continue with the program. Some parents allow the child to turn in earned stars for a bigger reward at the end of the week: a movie, for example.

5. Manage this system closely so the child feels successful in his efforts. Since this system demands new behavior from the child, it is important for the child to feel successful from the beginning or he will give up. Small, meaningful rewards work best to keep the excitement going.

When the system fails, it is usually because the parent fails to manage it consistently, and the excitement of earning rewards and praise becomes strained. So if parents are to attempt a token system, allow for the time and energy to manage it daily. If it is carried out efficiently over time, the child feels a sense of accomplishment at learning he can clean up and maintain his room and receive the praise of his parents.

A competing system of discipline is punishment. Punishment is the application of a negative response to the child's behavior. Common examples of punishment are spanking or demeaning the child. We discourage the use of punishment, either physically administered or emotionally applied in criticism or devaluation. While punishment may have a temporary suppressive effect on the child, years of research have shown it to have negative consequences on the child's confidence and ability to trust. The child can easily develop resentment toward the punisher. In short, punishment does not work very well beyond temporary control and should be reserved for extraordinary occasions, such as to prevent the child from endangering himself (running out in front of a car.) Even then, the use of punishment should be clearly explained so the child understands why it was used—for the child's safety and not to devalue the child as a person. It is important to keep in mind that parents often use punishment when they themselves are angry and the punishment satisfies their own anger. As a teaching technique, it does not add to the child's sense of security, trust, and positive self-image. Except for extraordinary circumstances, do not use physical punishment. Do not criticize, tease, or devalue your child with words.

Punishment and time-outs (sometimes called negative reinforcement) are not the same. Whereas punishment is the application of negative consequences to a child's behavior, a time-out is the removal of the opportunity to earn positive rewards. The child has the opportunity to earn back positive rewards by correcting the misbehavior. The emphasis of time out is on the correction the child needs. Placing the child in a time-out room (a room without rewards such as TV, computer, video games, etc.) following some misbehavior is the first step in the process. The essential part is helping the child to see what behavior he must change to return to positive family support.

So in conclusion, remember that discipline is teaching and you as the parent have ways to intervene with your child that can lead to success. Schor[1], et al., make these suggestions for changing the child's behavior:

1. Be selective about disciplining and keep things in perspective. Minor, irritating behavior should receive little parental attention.
2. Avoid these common mistakes:
   a. Parents may inadvertently punish good behavior or at least fail to reinforce good effort. For example, if their child improves her grades, raising them all to C's, parents may ask (inappropriately) "Why didn't you get B's?"

b. They may reward or reinforce bad behavior. This often occurs when a child continually whines or pleads and then the parent allows the child to get her way.
c. They may fail to reward good behavior. For instance, a child might wash the dishes and fail to be praised for accomplishing this task.
d. They may fail to stop a child's bad behavior or they may rationalize it. Perhaps one sibling is hurting another; the parent may respond, "Well, she deserved it," or "She needs to learn to fight back."

3. Reward and time-out specific behaviors. Focus on the behavior, and do not criticize the child as a person. (Do not say, "You are such a bad child.")
4. Use punishments sparingly and only when you are in control of your emotions. Physical punishment is harmful and not productive.
5. Children frequently experience physical and emotional distress, which can result in behavioral problems. Be sensitive to this issue, understand it, and try to eliminate the sources of the child's stress.
6. Some children exhibit behavioral problems because they have not been taught or have not experienced appropriate alternative behaviors. Teach them other, more acceptable, ways to behave and respond: "If you want money for a soda, ask me first; do not just take money from my purse."
7. Look beyond the concrete behavior the child is exhibiting and understand what she might be trying to tell you. Recognize that sometimes a child's worrisome behavior is a signal that she or the family is in pain. She may be the designated family

"messenger," and her behavior may be a cry for help for the entire family.

8. Recognize the state of your own emotions and your coping ability when confronting your child's behavior. That state may range from feeling competent and secure to feeling depressed and helpless. This recognition and self-awareness will help you decide if you need help or not and prevent an impulsive mistake.
9. Seek professional help when you think it is necessary. The earlier the intervention, the better the outcome. This professional input can also often provide reassurance that you are doing the right thing.

A Response to *Jimmy Eats the Snacks*

The principle to bear in mind is that Jimmy's misbehavior is an opportunity to teach him the values the family advocates. The first task is for dad to become aware of his own anger and not to act out his own emotion. Instead, dad should think of what he should say or do to set the stage for teaching. If dad is angry, sending Jimmy to his room until dad regains his teaching stance is preferable to spanking. Dad should see if this "stealing" is an isolated, impulsive act or part of a larger problem. Children have reasons for their actions. Does Jimmy feel deprived in some way, either of snacks or, in a larger sense, of feeling valued? Dad should dialogue empathetically with Jimmy to understand his thinking, get Jimmy to realize families share, and ask Jimmy to propose a solution to his own impulsive behavior. The family should support Jimmy's admission and change of behavior so that he will feel valued for cooperation and individual responsibility. It is part of the larger task of development of his conscience; i.e., internalization of social rules.

CHAPTER 9

Special Problems

Principle: Parents are advised to broaden their understanding of children's problem behaviors, learn how to listen, and effectively intervene so that over time the child develops internal controls: a conscience.

Cora Cheats on Her Social Studies Test

Cora has been a good student, and now in eighth grade she very much wants to attend a selective Jesuit high school and perhaps Notre Dame after that. Her teacher has called to say that on Cora's most recent social studies test, she was caught cheating by copying the paper of the boy seated next to her. You, her parents, are shocked and confused. The school wants to meet with you and Cora tomorrow.

You wonder: what should we say to Cora?

We have discussed discipline as teaching and suggested some methods that should produce not only situational control but also longer-term benefits. Yet we realize our children are constantly changing, growing up quickly. Growing up, moreover, is a bumpy road filled with obstacles and challenges. Even the parent who is thoughtful about her parenting, aware of her interventions, and harmonious with her spouse will encounter some turbulence with her child. The following is a brief discussion of commonly experienced problems.[1]

1. *Disobedience*

As parents we set the rules and expect our children to follow them. At times, however, they will defy these rules because they are testing these boundaries with their developing independence. At these times parents should employ the listening skills already discussed in chapter 3 to understand the child's behavior. While we want the child to learn self-control and observance of society's rules, we do not want to discourage her independent self-reliance. The end result we are aiming for is not only the child's ability to internalize rules to live as a good citizen, but also her ability to analyze situations so her obedience is reasonable for that situation; that is, we do not want simply blind obedience, but rather the child should be able to understand why she should follow the rule. This requires the parent's own understanding followed by a discussion of the importance of the rules. For example, cleaning up one's room is important for reasons of hygiene, order, and social appropriateness.

If you discover your child continually disobeys, you should try to understand her viewpoint: are your expectations unreasonable? Is she facing undue stress? Is she witnessing conflict in the family? All these situations can produce inner turbulence in a child that can manifest in resistance to authority. Children may not be able to adequately communicate these conflicts, so it is up to the parent to decipher the cause of the child's resistance. Often, when the child's problematic situation can be identified and resolved, the disobedience ceases.

It is helpful to see the role of the parent as that of a caring observer. The parent should know her child so well that she can sense when problems are present. Is the child overwhelmed? Is she reacting to the parent's anger or impatience? This sensitive intervention is an attempt to understand the child's pattern of behavior before it becomes hardened into habit. If the parent finds this problem-solving behavior too difficult, there are mental health experts who can help with these problems.

2. *Eating Disorders*[2]

Girls are susceptible to developing eating problems during the middle school years, and boys are not immune from these sorts of problems as well. Anorexia nervosa (characterized by a low weight or a failure to continue gaining weight during childhood) and bulimia nervosa (characterized by binge eating coupled with either self-induced vomiting, excessive exercising, or other ways of getting rid of calories) are the two primary eating disorders. But the vast majority of children and adolescents who have eating disorders experience a lesser version or a variation of the two main disorders. When a young person develops an eating disorder, she also can become withdrawn from family members or friends, and she also may be more irritable or more easily stressed out. Her sense of humor or interest in usual activities might fade. A child may develop an eating problem as a way of coping with low self-esteem, anxiety, stress, or depressed feelings, and it is important to talk to a mental health professional if you suspect that your child may have an eating problem.

Most eating disorders develop in the teenage years, and in middle school the foundations for these problems are being established. It is not uncommon to hear from your child that her friends are not eating lunch at school, and you'll notice that this can become contagious among groups of friends. If you hear that this is occurring, talk to your child about the importance of staying nourished throughout the day in order to have energy for school and activities. Do not hesitate to inform a teacher, the lunchroom monitor, and the principal of your concern as well so that they can address this issue early.

Signs to watch out for:

- Continuing concern with dieting—this could be cutting back on overall amounts of food (e.g., smaller portions), cutting out certain foods (e.g., ice cream), or skipping meals
- Obsessive reading of food labels
- Frequently not eating with the family (telling you, "I already ate"), or eating entirely different meals than what is prepared for the rest of the family
- Seeing or hearing evidence of vomiting after meals—for instance, going to the bathroom immediately after mealtimes
- Discovering large amounts of food missing
- Using diet pills, laxatives, or diuretics when these products are not needed

Steps you can take to prevent eating problems:

- *Prohibit any sort of weight-related teasing or criticism at home.* Parents or siblings may make well-intentioned comments about an overweight acquaintance's weight or tease a family member for being a "pig," but these sorts of comments create an environment of intolerance about weight. If there is a true medical concern about a child's eating habits in relation to being/becoming overweight, talk to your doctor or a mental health professional about ways to discuss this issue with sensitivity. Also, an excellent book for navigating eating and weight-related issues with your children is "*I'm, Like, So Fat": Helping Your Teen Make Healthy Choices about Eating and Exercise in a Weight-Obsessed World*," by Dianne Neumark-Sztainer.[3]

- *If you hear about a coach or a teacher teasing or criticizing your child or other children about their weight, talk to that coach or teacher, or complain to the principal.* Again, while these comments may not have been intended to be cruel, these attitudes only promote a hostile environment.
- *Prioritize regular evening family meals.* Busy schedules can make this difficult, and families often turn to allowing individuals to grab meals on their own or "on the go." But regular opportunities to sit down together to eat a meal allow for the provision of a healthy and well-balanced meal and promote communication among family members, as well as a sense of connectedness.[4] Creating that time together can ease the stress of the day and help to bring your values back into focus. In addition to reducing the risk of eating disorders, regular family meals (five or more per week) have been linked to reduced high-risk behaviors in adolescence like drug use, sexual activity, and violence. For more reading on this topic, see *Help Your Teenager Beat an Eating Disorder*, by Jim Lock and Daniel le Grange.[5]

3. *Aggressive Behavior*

We all must learn to control our aggressive impulses so as to live in an orderly and peaceful society. In the middle school years, boys more than girls are likely to express aggressiveness by violent means: hitting, destroying property, or bullying. Recently, however, there have been reports of girls bullying others, especially through cell or i-Phone communication. Schools are now adopting increasingly intolerant attitudes toward this kind of intimidation, so, now more than ever, it presents a challenge for parents to teach their children how to channel their aggressive impulses into socially acceptable activities. Usually this involves encouraging the child to understand his feelings and translate them into words which do not harm others. The goal is self regulation of emotions within society's standards.

What causes the child's aggression? As we try to understand the child's reactions, we can identify several common causes of aggression. First, a certain amount of aggression can be seen as a normal adjustment to the inevitable frustrations in confronting new and difficult situations. But some children have unusually intense temperaments or have inherited impulse control problems, such as ADHD (attention deficit hyperactivity disorder), which often involve severe frustration and result in the expression of aggressive impulses. Even without inherited conditions like ADHD, a family environment at times can be so stressful for the child that he is overwhelmed and deteriorates emotionally (a "melt-down") into aggression. Families who display impatience, intolerance, and aggression themselves may find their children imitating the parents' aggression. Or a child's aggression could arise from the parent's failure to teach the child self-control or setting limits through the use of time-outs and the encouragement of adaptive responses. And if the frustrated parent resorts to physical punishment of the child, he will model aggression as well as poor self-control, making matters even worse. Finally, a child's aggression may reflect a particular kind of stress, perhaps issues of neglect or abuse, which may in fact be a cry for help.

Aggression is also common among girls although usually expressed with less violence. Girls, particularly in middle school, will exclude other girls from their group's social activities, or talk about a particular girl unfavorably to others. The causes of this more subtle aggression may involve some of the above-mentioned causes but may also reflect poor socialization skills related to low self-esteem. It is often advisable for a girl to develop several networks of friends so that she need not be manipulated. For example, it is healthy for the middle school child to have different friends from her school, her sports program, and her church activities.

Parents can intervene effectively with problems of aggression using the same sensitive listening skills and understanding that we have discussed. Remember, a child wants his parents' approval, so expressing disappointment with the child's behavior can begin a productive discussion. The parent should try to get the child to understand how it feels to be on the receiving end of his aggression. It is certainly alright to generate some guilt in the child because we want him to internalize the reality that his aggression is unacceptable. He should come to understand that no one will like this behavior, and it is his job to manage these feelings by putting them into words. If the situation involves some perceived injustice, he should be guided to seek out the teacher or other person in authority to discuss it. Sometimes he may need a time-out, provide restitution, or apologize. In any of these situations, parents should reward the child's corrective efforts and reinforce his best efforts as being truly characteristic of him as a person.

4. *Stealing*

Parents may find at some point that their child will engage in some kind of stealing, lying, cheating, or even threatening to run away. By anticipating one or more of these events, parents can begin to teach their inappropriateness from an early age. In stealing, children in the middle years will sometimes take something not belonging to them as they become more independent and have not yet adapted fully to society's rules. They have not fully integrated the importance of recognizing that they may not take some toy or object belonging to another person. Particularly at about age seven and up, some children feel deprived in a material or emotional way. The act of stealing fills an emotional void, especially in cases where the child shares the spoils of his dishonesty with others. Older children may steal in response to peer pressure or in an effort to be accepted by a peer group. In all of these cases, the parent must confront the child and get him to understand that stealing is wrong, and that shame is an appropriate response. Because of the child's wish to earn parental approval, such explanations, without necessarily any additional punishment, should suffice. Stimulating a sense of guilt can be a useful tool because the parent is attempting to develop the child's conscience, and guilt is an internal confrontation of wrongdoing that can guide the child in the future. Usually the parent will require the child to make restitution or an apology to add to the corrective process. Do not state or imply that the child is a bad person. It is the specific behavior we are trying to correct while preserving the child's confidence in himself. One cautionary note: if stealing develops into a recurring pattern of behavior, then the parent should seek out a mental health consultation from a psychologist, social worker, or other appropriate specialist.

5. *Lying*

We want our children to tell the truth so that when the middle school child (of about ten or so) lies, he knows he is being deceitful. Most often he is lying because he is confronted with some behavior that he recognizes is wrong and feels afraid of parental disapproval or punishment. By lying, he believes he can hide his lapse. The parent must clearly explain to the child that lying is not acceptable. As with other disapproved behaviors, parents should intervene with sensitivity and support the child, but with a full understanding of the need to teach the child that telling the truth leads to people trusting one another, and lying undermines that trust. Also, lying gets the child into trouble. As with stealing, the role of the parent is to teach the correct behavior, so use the child's misbehavior as a lesson to prevent further mistakes. Finally, parents should be sufficiently aware of their own behavior regarding the truth and remember that children will imitate their parents.

6. *Cheating*

In our competitive society, we celebrate winners without giving appropriate attention to the hard work it takes to earn success. In this struggle to achieve, children will strive to meet their parents' expectations. If they discover that they fail to live up to these expectations, cheating can appear to be a convenient shortcut to take. Parents will see hints of this thinking in playing board games, sports, or other family activities. As with lying and stealing, parents need to discuss cheating as misbehavior and explain why cheating is dishonest. In an understanding and supportive manner, parents should redirect their energy into helping the child achieve, such as assistance with homework or finding a tutor. Rather than becoming angry, parents should see an incident of cheating as an opportunity to teach moral values in the most effective way possible.

7. *Swearing*

Most children will experiment with profane language as part of their emerging independence. Sometimes it is an attempt to appear sophisticated or to impress friends, but this tendency will fade if not rewarded, encouraged, or modeled in the family. Once again, discuss proper language with your child and what impression his language makes on others. Teach alternative ways of expressing oneself or other ways to cope with frustrations. Be aware of your own use of language.

7. *Running Away*

Running away from home is a serious expression of unhappiness and must be attended to immediately. Runaway children, especially preteens, are vulnerable to all kinds of ugly and dangerous exploitation. It can be prevented. Children who run away are usually expressing their inability to cope with personal or family stresses. Sometimes they expect overwhelming punishment from their parents, or they have come to feel they are a burden to their parents. Others are seeking adventure and naively believe running away will be a good time. At times the threat to run away may express the child's helplessness and desire to manipulate you. These situations call for careful intervention to understand what underlying issues are motivating the child. Nothing, however, justifies a parent's counter-threat daring the child to leave. When running away is encountered, it usually represents the proverbial tip of the iceberg of problems that have escaped your attention. It is not too late to understand the source of your child's desperation. With empathetic discussion, the child will usually reveal the tensions that are driving him, such as feeling neglected due to a divorce or custody battle, a sense of rejection from those who love him, or feelings of total failure. Most of these situations can be resolved, but if the parent is in the midst of his own turmoil or feels unable to confront these issues alone, getting a referral to a psychologist, social worker, or mental health therapist is appropriate.

A Response to *Cora Cheats on Her Social Studies Test*

In this situation, the parents are shocked that their daughter, who has exhibited exemplary behavior previously, has cheated. They need to discuss this misbehavior with her in a gentle but serious manner to understand why she chose a behavior so disparate with her usual manner. Did she feel the competition was overwhelming her? Did she feel unprepared in this subject? Did she fail to study for this test? Is there some other emotional burden she is bearing? Understanding her thinking will lead to its correction. Disappointment with herself and the disappointment she caused her parents may be enough of a negative outcome to move Cora toward correction. Parents should strive for correction of the situation as well as teaching Cora the proper principle to follow.

CHAPTER 10

Behavioral Problems Parents May Encounter

Principle: Parents may encounter any number of serious problems in their child or among their child's friends. It is helpful to understand what they mean, what conditions lead to these manifestations, and how best to intervene. Professional help is always an option. (A brief description of the specialties of a number of different professionals is provided at the end of this chapter.)

Tom's Concentration Problems

Tom is now in the seventh grade at Einstein Middle School and almost from the beginning he has had trouble concentrating and completing tasks. He loves activities like sports and outdoor games, but in the classroom he constantly fidgets and disturbs the other kids. Teachers have put him in a special classroom group, but even there he can't wait his turn. The other kids tease and sometimes avoid him. The principal calls you and wants to know whether he should be at Einstein at all.

How should you approach this problem?

One of the themes of this guide has been the importance of establishing and maintaining a continuous dialogue with your child. Only then can the parent evaluate the child's adaptation and progress in the many learning situations he faces. At the same time, this continuous contact provides the opportunity to teach the important messages parents have agreed upon to prepare the child for the road ahead. As we have described, the alert parent takes advantage of news events, family transitions, and movie or television programs to advance the healthy messages the parent wants to teach. Over time, these discussions should provide a firm structure for the values you want your child to possess.

In this section we want to describe several common problems parents might encounter with a child or among a child's friends. As in adult life, children face stressful situations every day when they strive to achieve in school and when they encounter children from different backgrounds and cultures. Most children from supportive families adjust reasonably well to new or different situations, but all children will encounter some obstacles. Here are several problem areas.

Teachers will report that some children exhibit behavioral problems. These behaviors depart from the social norm and signal a child's difficulties in adjustment to situations or other children's behavior. A child can become upset, display anger, or withdraw in sadness, often disrupting the classroom atmosphere. Usually these difficulties involve the child facing an emotionally overwhelming situation without the appropriate social tools to succeed. It can indicate some gap in the child's social preparation or reflect ongoing family stresses that are burdening the child. Most often the teacher's advice or the parent's suggestions are enough to get through the difficulty, but when these approaches are not enough, parents can consult a mental health specialist. Examples of behavioral problems include: the child who is used to winning or succeeding begins to lose or fail and has difficulty persevering; the child who feels left out or rejected by classmates or has difficulty adapting to new social situations like speaking in front of the class; or the child who withdraws emotionally when the family experiences some distress, such as a severe family disagreement or the serious illness of a loved one.

Whereas younger children may act out behaviorally or display psychosomatic distress such as a headache, stomachache, or even nightmares, middle or junior high students are more likely to become dispirited, irritable, disobedient, or withdraw from their usual activities. Often these troubled students experience a decline in achievement, and these emotional issues surface in parent-teacher conferences. It is essential for the parent to listen carefully to the student's viewpoint, extend support, and collaborate on an approach to resolve the problem. Often the teacher can contribute to improvement by rearranging the classroom situation to help the student gain support. Helping the student through this difficult situation can teach the child new responses to use in the future, and strengthens parent-child trust.

At times the child or one of his classmates may express his tensions in crude words or through an annoying habit. Parents should call attention to these behaviors and point out how negatively they are received and ask if this is how the young person wants to be recognized. Carefully observing the boundaries of responsibility for other people's children, the parent can present a corrective message in terms of the child's best behavior. That is, a parent can say, "Daniel, I bet you can say that in words your parents would be proud of. I know you can." Leading the child to realize which behaviors are self-defeating and which are constructive can produce positive growth without resorting to criticism. As parents, we should be on the lookout for opportunities to encourage this growth.

Depression affects everyone from one time to another, but when a child feels sad, hopeless, irritable, or withdrawn for weeks and months, then we must consider the possibility that the child is suffering from depression, an emotional disorder. Children become depressed for several reasons. Depression can be inherited from parents, or children could have been raised by depressed parents who have been unresponsive to their needs. Or the child could feel depressed as the result of a trauma such as child abuse, the loss of a significant relative or friend, or some sense of abandonment. Or the child may experience an extremely stressful situation like school failure, family problems, or difficulty with peers. In middle school, children will be more likely to describe themselves as sad, dumb, or a "loser." He may act in ways that suggest depression like withdrawing socially, especially from activities he once enjoyed. He may want to be alone or his grades may drop. Sometimes changes in appetite or sleep patterns can be detected, or he may complain of aches and pains and not want to go to school. Watch for signs of sadness, especially expressions of hopelessness, and also signs of excessive fatigue, poor concentration, or talk of hurting himself.

You can help your child by understanding what is contributing to his depression, acting in supportive ways and, if necessary, getting professional help. Help usually involves counseling and sometimes medication. Depressive symptoms should not be ignored because, over time, some children develop a hopelessness that leads to suicidal thinking. Middle schoolers rarely commit suicide, but teenagers do, and often the roots of their depression extend back to the middle years. Although the instances may be rare, be cautious if your child displays social withdrawal, sadness, and hopelessness; if he gives away prized possessions like his card collection or favorite sports memorabilia; or if a friend has committed suicide. Be sure to listen closely to your child and assess his ability to cope with the problems that may be overwhelming him. Do not ignore these symptoms.

It is likely your child will encounter someone with attention deficit hyperactivity disorder (ADHD). It is a disorder characterized by the child's distractibility and difficulty with concentration; impulsivity like acting without thinking or touching forbidden objects; inadequate ability to cope with frustration; and problems organizing, staying on task, or simply daydreaming. Boys tend to inherit ADHD more than girls, and these children experience difficulty getting along with peers as well as persevering in school tasks. Perhaps as a result of their inability to succeed, they often suffer from low self-esteem despite the fact that ADHD and level of ability are not related. ADHD is not diagnosed before age six or seven.

ADHD with hyperactivity is easier to identify because the child usually fidgets, squirms, or is restless. Some describe the child as "restless," a "revving engine," or "bouncing off the walls." He lacks patience, can hardly wait his turn, and often fails at tasks requiring organization or follow-through. ADHD without hyperactivity is characterized by inattention, carelessness, poor listening skills, and disorganization. He loses things, forgets, and is disorganized. Children with ADHD often feel like failures in traditional school settings, and unless this disorder is diagnosed early, they tend to experience school as unrewarding and are at risk of dropping out. These children need to be treated by a medical or psychological expert. An accurate diagnosis must come from an accumulation of data on the child, and treatment usually involves a behavioral approach involving the parents as close managers of the child's behavior, and may involve medication as well. ADHD continues into adolescence and adulthood, although by self-selection, children with ADHD often find occupations or areas of study that call for abilities somewhat different from those emphasized in school.

A common disorder parents may encounter with their child or with their child's friend is stuttering. Most children who stutter tend to improve by high school, but stuttering can distress parents. To provide the most constructive intervention, parents should first be patient. In this frame of mind, parents should use their common sense and encourage conversations that are not too stressful for the child to be able to practice vocal control. Be encouraging and allow him to proceed at his own pace and assure him that his efforts will eventually lead to progress. As with other interventions with our children, do not interrupt, criticize, or punish. If these efforts do not achieve improvement over time, consult a speech pathologist.

Unfortunately, parents must be sensitive to signs of child abuse and neglect. It is alarming that abuse and neglect of children are so prevalent, but it is better that we all recognize the vulnerability of children and respond constructively rather than remain ignorant of their occurrence. It is widely reported that girls are more likely to be sexually abused than boys, but if we include in our definition of abuse, emotional and physical abuse, boys are just as vulnerable. Often dysfunctional families will abuse in all these ways. Physical abuse is perhaps the most visible form of abuse because certain bruises, human bite marks, or cigarette burns are seldom, if ever, accidents. Parents should be particularly watchful if these marks are on parts of the body usually unharmed in sports or spirited play, such as cheeks, stomach, or buttocks. If the child appears unusually aggressive, expresses fear of a parent or caretaker, or is secretive and guarded about his injuries, parents should be suspicious. Knowing the families of your child's friends can be enormously helpful in these situations. Does the family suffer serious emotional distress, remain socially isolated, or suffer from the effects of alcohol or substance abuse? Does the child express advanced or premature sexual knowledge beyond her years, indicate sexual promiscuity, or remain uncomfortably secretive about family relationships? Emotional abuse is perhaps the most common form of abuse. If the child is continually belittled, ridiculed, or harshly criticized, this could constitute emotional abuse. Try to be fair minded in your observations because it is difficult to distinguish between true abuse and occasional intemperate responses.

Parents must be constantly vigilant and protective of children. Even with one's own family, a parent should be sensitive to how affection is demonstrated, and should be aware if a child feels coerced into an uncomfortable response. Your daughter may not want to kiss Uncle Chuck good-bye or your son may not benefit from Grandfather Bryant's "manly" expectations. Observe all relationships carefully and be sure your child feels free to tell you of any situation in which he or she feels uncomfortable. Believe your child and investigate carefully. Protecting the child is a parent's first duty, but inquiries must be sensitive and fair. You can then devise a clear message and strategy for your child or remove your child from the problematic situation altogether.

The identification of abuse in a friend of your child is obviously a sensitive situation. If the child displays the signs of abuse described above, a parent may choose to tactfully inquire of the child's family if they are aware of their child's distress. If the parent seems responsive and supports the child, the inquiry may draw a positive response. If the inquiry provokes a self-protective denial, anger, or some unusual defensiveness, a referral to child protective services may be in order. Teachers, doctors, and professionals are mandated to report potential abuse, so the situation may have been noticed by others as well. However, if you as a parent believe the child is being abused and no one else has taken action, you should call the state's child protective service to file a report. Child safety must be our primary concern.

A Response to *Tom's Concentration Problems*

There could be a number of reasons for Tom's poor concentration and hyperactivity. If parents have discussed these adjustment problems with Tom previously and there has been no correction, it is time to have him evaluated by a clinical psychologist. These symptoms appear to be attention deficit hyperactivity disorder, but only a careful evaluation can rule out other sources of tension that could result in the same symptoms. Tom and his family may benefit from counseling in this case, and with such a diagnosis the school can make special accommodations to improve Tom's learning situation.

There are several kinds of professionals upon whom we rely:

1. Psychiatrists are medical doctors who have post-medical school specialization in various areas. For our purposes we would look for a child psychiatrist or one with a specialty in helping families. Psychiatrists are especially trained to treat serious illnesses and prescribe medications for conditions such as severe depression, including suicidal behavior, bipolar illness, attention deficit disorder, and serious anxieties.
2. Psychiatric nurses are nurses who have a specialty in treating psychiatric disorders with medication. Look for those nurses with experience with children and adolescents.
3. Psychologists have a PhD (PsyD or EdD) in psychology, the science of human behavior. They are experts in human development and behavior and competent in treating learning, behavioral, and emotional disorders. Like psychiatrists, psychologists have various specialties such as child and family, but unlike psychiatrists they are not medical doctors and thus do not prescribe medication.

They usually can evaluate conditions through testing and offer specialized therapy programs.

4. Some pediatricians have behavioral and developmental specialties that involve children with behavioral and emotional problems and a range of behavioral and neurological difficulties. They can prescribe medication.
5. Mental health counselors are practitioners who treat family and child problems. Counselors usually have two years of postgraduate training, either a master's degree in social work, or a master's degree in counseling. The individual's specialty and training should be the important aspect of the counselor's background to examine when selecting someone at this level of training.
6. Community agencies such as community mental health centers, or religiously affiliated agencies such as Catholic Community Services provide community mental health services to a broad population and offer a variety of services, especially to low-income clients.

CHAPTER 11

Internet Safety

by Angela Celio Doyle, PhD, clinical associate in the department of psychiatry and behavioral neuroscience, University of Chicago

Principle: Families can control some stress in their lives with preventive thinking and careful vigilance regarding Internet use.

Sarah's Online "Friend"

Your twelve-year-old daughter Sarah loves playing on the home computer, and she and her friends are beginning to use a social networking website, Facebook. You find out from another parent that Sarah has been communicating online with a new "friend": a twenty-two-year-old man, who contacted Sarah when he saw her picture on her online profile.

What do you do?

One of the themes of this guide has been to become a self-aware and thoughtful parent so as to put forth your best effort to prepare your child for the challenges she will face. Another way of stating this goal is to use vigilance to prevent unfortunate circumstances from occurring. Parents agree that observing certain rules of safety can prevent conflict and suffering, so this section will highlight a particular hazard in today's world: the Internet. According to the Pew Internet and American Life Project, 93 percent of American teenagers use the Internet.[1] It is a valuable tool and one that plays an increasingly important presence in your child's educational and social lives. However, the Internet presents several hazards that require attention from parents, particularly as their children progress through middle school into junior high and high school.

First, you may be concerned about your child accessing websites that are inappropriate, such as those about drugs or alcohol or even pornography. These websites are very easy to access, so your child might find them accidentally or seek them out because she is curious. There are several options for limiting your child's access to certain websites, including blocking software, which blocks prespecified websites that you select, and filtering software, which screens out websites and parts of websites that include certain phrases or terms that you prespecify. If you are uncertain about what websites your child is visiting, talk to her about her usage. If you are still anxious, you can check by viewing the "history" in the web browser on your computer (e.g., Internet Explorer, Mozilla Firefox).

Second, in an unmonitored Internet environment, it is possible for "cyber-bullying" to take place among peers. Instant messaging is a feature that has become popular among adolescents, as well as social networking websites such as MySpace, Facebook, Twitter, and others. While these sites can allow for opportunities for adolescents to creatively express themselves and to communicate with their classmates at school, it is also possible for teasing or bullying to take place. If you become aware that your child—or another child—is being targeted online, consider contacting the parents of the child who is doing the online bullying as well as the principal of your child's school.

The principal and teachers will want to address the issues of Internet safety and bullying with the larger student body.

Third, the Internet makes it easy to communicate with strangers, which increases the risk of victimization through identity theft or predators connecting with your child. You have likely had a conversation with your child when she was younger about sharing private information, such as her address or date of birth, with strangers, so a conversation about how these same rules apply to interactions online will make sense. The most common ways that your child may be approached for these kinds of information are through e-mails directly sent to her or through "chat rooms" or other social message boards found on a website. Sharing an e-mail address among family members during middle school allows for monitoring the kinds of e-mails that arrive for your child and provides opportunities for discussion. On social networking sites such as Facebook, it is possible to block personal information from being viewed by the general public. Although you may not be personally interested in these social networking websites, get to know them as well as you can and become especially familiar with the privacy settings in order to work with your child to limit what information is available to the public. It is wise to allow interactions only with people identified as "friends"—preferably people who are already acquaintances in real life. Additionally, social networking sites often have a function where "alerts" are sent to a prespecified e-mail address when certain actions are taken. For instance, when a person contacts your child to become an online "friend," an e-mail can be directed to your e-mail account so that you may monitor this.

Here are some additional suggestions to prevent Internet-related problems:

1. **Learn more about the Internet**. If you are not an active Internet user, speak to a friend of the family

or a relative who is Internet savvy to learn more about the current technology and the risks associated with the Internet. Ask your child to explain what she knows to you. There are also books on the topic, such as *Cyber-Safe Kids, Cyber-Savvy Teens: Helping Young People Learn to Use the Internet Safely and Responsibly* by Nancy Willard.

2. **Keep computers out of the bedrooms and in a public space in the house**. Having computer use easily observed can reduce the likelihood of Internet activities that put your child at risk. If you have laptops or cell phones with Internet capabilities, putting guidelines on when and where these are used can be important.
3. **Protect private information**. Talk to your child about the importance of not sharing her full name, address, phone numbers, school name, date of birth, photographs, or other information that could allow a stranger to locate her.
4. **Share an e-mail account**. A family e-mail account can help in monitoring your child's internet activity. Also, it allows for discussion of the risks as well as the more enjoyable aspects of the Internet such as humorous e-mails or updates from far-off relatives.
5. **Talk about what websites your child visits and Internet activities your child is engaging in**. You can also check the "history" of online use in your website browser if you are unsure of what sites your child is accessing.
6. **Know whom your child is interacting with online**. Just as in real life, it is wise to know who your child's friends are to reduce the risk of her becoming involved with inappropriate people.

7. **Restrict certain websites that you are uncomfortable with**. In addition to blocking and filtering software, most Internet providers allow you to set "parent controls" that can limit the websites your child is able to access. Call your Internet provider for more information on this feature.
8. **Limit overall computer use**. Social connections can be supplemented by computer use, just as phone calls used to be a main way for adolescents to keep in touch, but in-person socializing is a much better way to help with your child's social development.

A Response to *Sarah's Online "Friend"*

There are many opportunities to help your children become more Internet savvy during middle school through involvement and discussion about risky situations. Parents should closely monitor their children's online activities and "meet" their online friends. Sarah's parents allowed her to keep her Facebook page but used the Facebook security options to block her picture and profile to others who did not already know her. Her "friendship" with the twenty-two-year-old man was ended, and the man was told to stay away.

CHAPTER 12

The Importance of Family

Principle: Maintaining a healthy family means attending not only to parenting, but achieving a satisfying career and an enriching life as a couple.

Mike and Marla

Mike and Marla worked hard to be effective parents. They set clear goals and values for their children, helped with homework, coached sports teams, and achieved in their respective careers. Yet they found themselves becoming irritable and frustrated, blaming each other for jobs not done. One day Daniel, their eight-year-old son, asked them, "Why do you guys argue so much?" Mike and Marla looked at each other with dawning awareness.

What do you think this awareness was?

In a world of conflict and confusion, our family is our bulwark and refuge. Members of our family comprise our primary relationships and essential connections with our unique identities and cultural heritage. Families provide protection and security so that members may learn about capabilities relative to the outside world. We need to care for our families, to support one another.

There is no typical family today. Although most are still traditional two-parent families, many are single parent or blended families, and some are multigenerational families. Recent trends even note young adults living at home longer than in previous generations, so emerging adults have added a new dimension to our idea of families.

Although children can be successfully raised in a variety of different family configurations, recent studies support the findings of a report by the National Conference of State Legislators: "Children living with two biological parents tend to have better cognitive and emotional development and school achievement than children living with a single parent. Children raised in single-parent homes are at greater risk of poverty, juvenile delinquency and teen pregnancy and are more likely to divorce as adults."[1] All things being equal, then, it is best for children to be raised by their two biological parents. However, life is often not optimal, and it is essential that the adults in a child's life—whether biological or step-parents, whether a single mother or father or a grandparent—realize that their interactions with the child will impact every aspect of their child's life. Healthy and happy relationships in the home, and enrollment in a supportive school with a strong community, can alleviate many of the potential disadvantages of a nontraditional family setting.

In most cases a man and a woman who are parents of school-age children function as a couple to head a family. Family leadership is important because the first task we discussed in better parenting was to define the family's goals and values and model these values for our children. Yet we know living closely with someone is a challenge and requires continuous self-examination. This work is essential to our self-awareness and the consistent transmission of value-laden messages. It is plain to see that the same qualities of empathetic communication described in chapter 3 should also apply to a couple. The ability to listen accurately and respectfully to another person's viewpoint is as important as the clear articulation of personal values. In other words, you as a couple are a team that must confront the daily problems of growing children. If you are in disarray, family management will become impossible.

This is why counselors, pastors, and experienced parents all agree that couples must set aside time for one another. Couples have three primary functions in family life: the role as a parent is obvious as you meet your children's daily needs. The role as an individual is apparent as you go to work in your chosen career every day and perhaps even enjoy special pastimes or hobbies. The role most neglected, however, is your role as a two-person loving couple. Somehow couples often let this vital connection slip and, as a result, the compelling reasons you came together in the first place can be lost. The emotional enrichment, the intellectual stimulation, and loving support that everyone needs must be maintained. Take time for it. Make plans to spend time together.

Balancing these three roles will go a long way to maintaining a couple's emotional health and, thus, strengthening their ability to meet the challenges of parenting. We have spent some time now on suggestions about parenting. We have emphasized setting a consistent structure, daily routines around which parents can sensitively intervene with their children. These provide numerous teaching opportunities children will need if they are to learn the family's goals and values.

Parents will need to work diligently to succeed in their careers. Not only is earning an income necessary to meet the realistic demands of daily life, but a parent's own self-esteem and worth are important to maintain for authority and confidence. It is healthy, moreover, for children to see parents enjoying life with their hobbies, friendships, and pursuits that bring them happiness. Celebrating every family member's birthday, religious holidays, and special occasions provide bonding memories for every family member.

Equally important to model to the children is a loving relationship, a clear idea of what a committed relationship is supposed to be. In chapter 5 we noted a daughter's favorable impression of her father as a template for her idea of a loving partner. Boys as well see their mothers portraying similar loving qualities. Failure to develop such a relationship deprives children of healthy models to strive for and deprives parents of a crucial source of life's satisfactions. We all need this balance.

A healthy family, then, is the train we ride in raising our children. If we take time and make efforts to maintain it, we can advance our lives in the positive direction we first envisioned in our dreams for the future for ourselves and our children.

A Response to *Mike and Marla*

This perceptive couple began to realize their own relationship had eroded through neglect. They had not made time for each other to talk, to touch, to connect with their loving feelings for one another. By spending this more intimate time together, they could regain a deeper appreciation for each other and work more effectively together as well.

Epilogue

So there you have it. These twelve principles, if consistently applied, should help guide you as you encounter the many challenges of shaping your child's development. Parenting is a difficult job, but if we have a clear direction and live out our values, we can achieve the satisfactions of a loving and supportive family. A few years ago there was an African saying, "It takes a village to raise a child," that became one of the most popular catchphrases of the day. Many educational reform efforts began with the phrase and a book by the wife of a U.S. president took the beginning of the phrase as its title. The phrase caught the public imagination because we all realize our children learn not only from us as parents, but also from their many associations—teachers, coaches, pastors, friends, and society's institutions, particularly schools. As parents, we hope they are most influenced by those people with values similar to our own. Parents who have made the effort to send their children to schools that are consistent with their family values are more likely to feel a sense of satisfaction with their experience. In this sense, we believe our children are best prepared to become productive and thoughtful citizens in our society.

At times, parents may encounter problems that are too difficult to solve by themselves. I have mentioned several examples in this book and indicated where professional help may be needed. Your pastor, principal, pediatrician, or family doctor are all acquainted with professionals who are trained and skillful in providing help to parents. These professionals are usually doctors with specialized training in family problems and child development. They offer consultation to you and your child by the hour in confidential appointments. Parents who seek out these professionals will at first present the problem, provide the family's historical background, and develop with the professional's assistance a strategy to resolve the problem. Your feelings of trust in his expertise and personal comfort with his responses are essential to begin this process. Parents should remember they have a choice of experts, and selecting someone with whom they can work successfully should be the first task (someone who advocates the principles in this book, for example). If you establish this rapport, be prepared to trust him with your personal information so he can tailor a program that addresses the causes of the problem.

After carefully listening to the problem and asking relevant historical questions, he will outline his therapeutic plan for your approval. He will offer some initial explanations but will want to involve you as a family to work collaboratively to resolve the problem. Counseling or psychotherapy is hard work and usually involves relearning self-defeating habits over a number of weeks. Many people have benefited from counseling, especially when it has helped to improve our individual self-awareness and faulty patterns of interacting with one another.

A wise man once said you can tell the health of a tree by the beauty of its fruit. Our children are the fruit of both our union and the care we have taken to produce these excellent young men and women. Our lives present many opportunities for fulfillment, but is there any more satisfying accomplishment than successfully raising a thoughtful, caring, and ethical son or daughter? If parents invest their best efforts in the directions we have outlined in this book, they will find an unmatched sense of satisfaction. It will manifest increasingly over time and culminate in a number of memorable moments. One such moment will be your child's high school graduation, when you will witness a completion: a young man or woman who has mastered intellectual challenges, succeeded in varied and diverse relationships, and chosen a future path for greater growth. Your child will not yet be a finished product, but watching him standing there in graduation robes, you will realize the beautiful bloom of youth, soundly taught and well prepared for the future. I envy you that moment.

Ten Scenarios for Practice

I hope you have read this book on parenting with the important assumption that we are not and will not be perfect parents. We all make mistakes in raising our children, but if we are clear in what we value, transmit our desire to be an attentive listener to the child's viewpoint, and provide wise, corrective guidance, we will have done the job we had hoped for. When wise parents make mistakes, they correct them as part of their self-reflection, and they realize that over time there will be literally thousands of opportunities to transmit messages about the values they believe are important for a satisfying and happy life.

If you have read this book carefully, you should have an approach to parenting that can begin to guide you in a healthy direction. As I said earlier, these principles have been "field tested" on our own children, children in my child and family practice, and with many other parents with whom we have talked over the years. So now gather up your healthy sense of humor, your thoughtful judgment, and your acquired wisdom to play the role of parenting advisor. I will present ten situations for you to evaluate in a quiz we are calling: Mastering the Art of Parenting.

Here are ten scenarios from typical family life together with four possible parenting responses. After reading each scenario, decide which is the best intervention (based on the principles defined in this book) and compare your answers with those that we offer. Score one point for each "correct" answer, or score a point for any choice if you can provide a healthy rationale consistent with the principles in this book. We trust your self-scoring ability. A perfect score is a ten.

Scenario 1: Horse Sense

Peter and Paula grew up on horse farms and loved horses. They introduced their only child, Jean Marie, to riding and horse care at an early age, and Jean Marie appeared to have a genuine and immediate affinity for riding. Even at age eight, she was appearing in horse shows and competitions and began to win trophies for her riding skill. At ages ten and eleven, Jean Marie became the state champion rider for her age group, and she was featured in a number of statewide magazines and newspapers along with pictures and articles about her family. If she continued along this path, all the papers said, Jean Marie was sure to attract scholarships from colleges and perhaps even earn a tryout for the Olympic games. Peter and Paula received much praise from their community and were proud of Jean Marie. Then one day just after her twelfth birthday, Jean Marie told her parents she was tired of horses and refused to participate in any more riding competitions. Shocked at this sudden change of heart about what had defined all of their lives, Peter and Paula wondered how they should respond to Jean Marie.

What would you advise?

A. Recognize that girls' interests change. Give up the riding and encourage Jean Marie to begin a new activity or interest.
B. Point out the enormous benefits she would be giving up at this point and strongly urge Jean Marie to keep riding even if she did not enjoy it.
C. Begin a series of discussions about the benefits and liabilities of continuing to ride. Convey some of your leanings on both sides of the issue, but

convey to Jean Marie that ultimately she herself would have to make a well-thought-out choice.

D. Call a local psychologist who specializes in adolescent issues and meet as a family.

A Response to *Horse Sense*

First of all, we hope Peter and Paula have continually maintained a supportive and open dialogue with Jean Marie and have discussed why she continues to participate. Is it enjoyable for her? Does she value the social learning beyond the riding? Does she feel good about the attention she receives? As Jean Marie's parents, they hope to translate this activity into her overall development as a person. They are careful to reflect on their own gratification derived from Jean Marie's success and separate this feeling from the benefits Jean Marie receives (the primary goal of the activity). Through ongoing discussions they reach a decision that they all believe to be in Jean Marie's best interests. Peter and Paula are attentive listeners to Jean Marie, and she feels they have acted in her best interests.

The panel, therefore, voted for Option C. If you chose this option, award yourself a point. Option A, on the other hand, recognizes changing attitudes in adolescence, but appears to minimize the importance of Jean Marie's years of investment and its importance to her self-esteem. Option B suggests advocating the parents' wishes, which override Jean Marie's wishes and risks creating a conflict that may morph into more incendiary conflicts later. Option D is an acceptable alternative—so award yourself a point for this choice if it facilitates the same points as option C, but be cautious that it could suggest putting the responsibility of the decision onto another person. (See principles 1, 2, 3, 5.)

Scenario 2: A Loaded Gun

Kate and John are family practice doctors who have prided themselves in serving patients who do not have access to regular medical care. They commute daily from a suburb to a rural area in order to serve people in a less affluent county. Both Kate and John grew up in rural areas and have frequently brought their son, Matt, age twelve, and daughter, Melissa, age ten, to the mountains, where they have a cabin and enjoy hiking and outdoor life as a family. One day Kate looks for a book she lent to Matt and discovers hidden under his bed a loaded rifle. This discovery shocks her because they have never had firearms in the house, at least to her knowledge. She tells John and they have a discussion with Matt, who has seemed increasingly withdrawn and irritable over the last several months. John asks Matt how he intends to use the rifle but gets only a silent reply. John asks about a dead cat he found in their yard a few weeks ago, but Matt claims he knows nothing about it. Kate remembers that Matt's teacher left several phone messages two weeks ago, but this occurred at a time when they both had medical emergencies, and the calls were never returned. Matt tells his parents to just leave him alone.

What would you advise the parents?

A. Ignore all this—Matt is going through a phase of independence. Take the ammunition from him and schedule some hunting activities.

B. Take this seriously: the signs point to a potential disaster. The parents have been emotionally out of touch with Matt; he is isolated and perhaps having trouble in school; and his mood is irritable and withdrawn, classic signs of depression. And there is the question of a dead animal. Call for psychiatric evaluation.

C. They should sit down with Matt and ask him to be reasonable as they have always tried to be. Doesn't he realize that someone could get hurt with a loaded rifle?

D. Kate and John should consider their work patterns and lifestyle and how it has affected their children. Perhaps they need more vacation time to deal with all the tension.

A RESPONSE TO *A LOADED GUN*

We all get busy with our lives, and at times we can lose touch with the developing feelings within our children. In this case, two well-meaning and dedicated professionals who have sacrificed a lot to be able to contribute to their community appear to have lost touch with their son's frustrations, his depression, and possible suppressed rage. His emotional withdrawal, irritability, and possible school difficulty appear to have been neglected by these busy parents. The loaded rifle is a literal and metaphorical description of the anger involved and calls for an immediate intervention. That is why the panel chose option B with its obvious social awkwardness and its anxieties about what an evaluation will produce. The evaluation is likely to lead to a more sustained family involvement in examining the nature of relationships in the family. Option A, of course, ignores the danger signals. Option C might have helped some time ago, but that juncture has passed. Immediate help is necessary. And option D also may have helped, years ago. (See principles 3, 4, 6, 10.)

Scenario 3: The Runaway

Woody and Jane were fun to be around—their children, Lizzie and Jimmy, even said so. They presented the kind of family that drew the friends of their children, even some kids they had never met, to their home. Kids were usually there after school and on weekends, and Jane would always have some popcorn or Kool-Aid on hand to welcome their guests. There were plenty of games, from basketball in the driveway to Trivial Pursuit on the floor of the family room. Even Woody was surprised when he saw Jane announce it was cleanup time and every child followed orders without hesitation. One evening at about ten p.m., there was a knock on the door. Standing there with a duffle bag in her hand was Lizzie's seventh-grade friend Susan, looking exhausted, bedraggled, and depressed. Susan told Jane she was running away from home but wanted to spend the night. Jane could see that Susan had been crying and was in no condition to talk. She arranged a comfortable place for her to sleep near Lizzie, and while making up a bed, she heard Susan's description of a bitter family argument culminating in her father's telling her to "get lost—we didn't want you in the first place!" Jane tried to calm her and get her to sleep. Jane talked with Woody about what to do. She was able to get a message to Susan's parents assuring them Susan was safe, but what should she do next?

What advice would you give Jane?

A. In the morning, Jane should call Susan's parents and tell them it was time to pick up Susan without mentioning anything about the family dispute.
B. In the morning Jane should call Susan's parents and ask about their family problems and advise them on how to handle Susan.
C. In the morning when Susan has rested, Jane should try to begin a discussion about her crisis. Explain that every family has problems and go over some alternatives until Susan agrees on a healthy direction to take.

D. In the morning Jane should call Child Protective Services and report this incident.

A Response to *The Runaway*

While we all admire the warm hospitality of Woody and Jane's home, we do not envy their being thrust into a family squabble they know little about. They should proceed cautiously, first calming and listening to Susan's version of what the conflict is about, the ability of her parents to address it, and the possibility of abuse of some kind. It is likely Susan is overwhelmed and would allow Jane to call or visit her parents (or the parent Susan prefers) to assure them she is doing better and to inform them of the depth of upset Susan feels. Gauging their response and trying to minimize defensiveness, Jane might ask if she could make a suggestion Susan has endorsed: to refer them to a friend who is a family counselor. Even if the parents reject this offer, they should realize the seriousness of the situation and that it has been noticed by others in the community. It is hoped that Jane can determine if it is safe for Susan to return home. For these reasons the panel chose option C, whereas option A would ignore Susan's feelings and possibly cut off her safe approach to problem-solving. Option B suggests the high potential for insensitivity to a complex family situation, and option D, while appropriate if there is evidence of abuse, might in this case be an overreaction. (See principles 3, 5, 10.)

Scenario 4: The Biased Teacher

Jose and Maria tolerated it for a while, but after the latest parent-teacher conference with Mr. Leipzig, their daughter Anna's seventh-grade teacher, they were upset. They found Mr. Leipzig unusually critical of Anna's essays, her class participation, and her behavior. Anna was a smart girl who had sailed through grades one through six with glowing comments from all her teachers. While seventh grade was a new experience, they sensed something more was going on than adjusting to a new environment. Anna and her girlfriends complained that Mr. Leipzig played favorites, liked the boys more than the girls, and if he responded positively to a girl, it would be the pretty blond girls who dressed with all the feminine touches. The boys, of course, loved him, and there were lots of games and attention with Mr. Leipzig. When Anna's grades fell from her usual 4.0 to 2.9 grade point average and several parent-student-teacher conferences produced no positive changes, Jose and Maria were at their wits' end.

What should they do?

A. Organize a group of dissatisfied parents and confront Mr. Leipzig about his possibly discriminatory behavior.
B. Ignore this situation and get through the year. Eighth grade will be better for Anna.
C. Document examples of Mr. Leipzig's preferential treatment and seek out the principal to describe their dissatisfaction and to find ways to resolve it.
D. Ask for a change of teachers, and if that is impossible, look into that private religious school nearby.

A Response to *The Biased Teacher*

There is no question that in most cases teachers are dedicated and caring individuals who work hard to contribute to our children's education. But teachers are as human as we are, and they at times have problems that distort their efforts. In this case, Mr. Leipzig may have failed to examine his interactive style with girls, and this has contributed to the perception of favoritism. If

Jose and Maria have specific examples of this behavior, and if their meetings with Mr. Leipzig have not produced any progress, then taking their concerns to the principal would be appropriate. The tone of this meeting should be problem solving, not confrontation, and the primary goal should be the best educational situation for Anna. Implications for other students should be obvious as well. The principal should be equally interested in what is best for Anna, and it should be expected that the principal has handled parental dissatisfaction before. Some adjustment in Anna's situation should come from this meeting. For these reasons, the panel chose option C. If the principal refuses to make any changes that will help Anna's learning, then option D would be a reasonable course. Option B could produce discomfort and discouragement for Anna that might affect her established motivation for achievement. Option A may resemble a protest that might mobilize resistance to Jose and Maria's cause. (See principles 1, 4.)

Scenario 5: Like Father, Like Son?

Everywhere Ted went in town, people would recognize him as the outstanding quarterback he had been. Ted had been all-conference at Michigan and even played three seasons for the Detroit Lions before an injury ended his career. Ted now coached youth football, and men sought out his advice about developing their sons into outstanding athletes. But Ted's motivation in coaching was to develop his own son, Ted Jr., into a stellar football player. Ted played catch with him, taught him plays and football strategy, and even took him to all the Michigan home games. Ted Jr., however, had inherited his mother's coordination, and despite his dad's mentorship, Ted Jr., was only an average athlete. He clearly wanted to please his dad, emulate him, and carry on the family tradition in which they all took pride. His abilities, however, were clearer in his studies and in drawing. Now the high school coach was rounding up boys for a summer camp in which Ted knew he would be scouting for the boys who would make the varsity team. Ted knew Ted Jr. would not stand out as a star. Confidentially, Ted discussed his pessimism with his wife. Should he discourage Ted Jr. from attending the camp? Ted Jr. said he wanted to go, but Ted feared his son would experience disappointment.

What would you advise the parents?

A. Keep your pessimism to yourself, let him attend, and let the chips fall where they may.
B. Have Ted talk with the coach and perhaps influence him to select Ted Jr. who, after all, is a "late bloomer."
C. Find a drawing workshop and encourage that activity so Ted Jr. can develop his talent.
D. Discuss with Ted Jr. the challenges and issues of self-development, including achieving success and experiencing failure both as part of overall success.

A Response to *Like Father, Like Son*?

As parents we harbor dreams for our children, sometimes in a particular field or activity. Ted undoubtedly wanted his son to enjoy the successes he had enjoyed. But the larger picture is Ted Jr.'s unique self-development so that the path he chooses will produce satisfaction and happiness for himself. While wanting to please his parents, Ted Jr. would be fortunate if his parents experienced pride and praise for whatever Ted Jr. chose. That is, there is no one path or activity they would expect him to follow. In this case, we recommend that Ted encourage his son to try out for the football camp and put forth his best effort. There is a reasonable likelihood he would make the team with hustle and good attitude even if only as a backup player. But at the same time, the parents should encourage other activities, both academic and artistic, to broaden his experience and to show there are many ways to develop competence and confidence. The panel chose option D for these reasons. Option A does not provide any preparation for Ted Jr. for what is to come, and he may experience a disappointment that he is unprepared for. Option B sounds too intrusive and overprotective and could backfire, leaving Ted Jr. exposed to a negatively prejudiced decision. Option C might give Ted Jr. the message that he should change directions, and that he has failed his father. (See principles 1, 3, 6.)

Scenario # 6: The Beer Party in Room 12

Benjamin loved his i-Phone and used it every day. He enjoyed taking photographs of his friends, and his friends enjoyed taking pictures of each other. One day after seventh-grade study hall, when everyone else was attending an all-student assembly, Benjamin and his friend Curt took photos of each other—as a joke—with an empty can of Budweiser they had found. Soon the photo of a grinning Benjamin with the can of Budweiser in his hand was all over school, and classmates were calling it, "the beer party in room twelve." The principal was incensed and called Benjamin's parents to set up a meeting with them and Benjamin to "determine the consequences."

What would you advise Benjamin's parents to do?

A. Dispute the validity of the photo. After all, these photos can be easily distorted. Benjamin could have been manipulated into this misbehavior, and the principal should let it go.
B. Make it clear to Benjamin he has humiliated the entire family, and he is in for some harsh discipline. He will have to demonstrate to others in the

community he is really sorry for bringing shame and humiliation to their family name.

C. Discuss the event with Benjamin to find out what really happened and what Benjamin thinks his response should be. Be clear that as parents, they are on his side, but there must be some corrective response.

D. Make plans to move from the community, perhaps to Canada.

A Response to *The Beer Party in Room 12*

We all know how modern technology—i-Phones, Twitter, and the use of Facebook, and MySpace—has changed the nature of communication. Impulsive decisions can be spread widely and instantly, so much so that their potential for embarrassment, or worse, calls for some instruction. Everyone makes mistakes in judgment, even adults, so this episode can provide a valuable lesson for Benjamin in determining how to behave and whom to trust. In the larger scheme of things, this one situation is less important for its embarrassment than for the caution he will learn to bring to such situations in the future. The panel chose option C: utilize this opportunity to have a reasonable and supportive discussion with Benjamin, who is already experiencing negative consequences of his behavior. He should be taught that an honest and reasonable approach in problem solving will serve him best socially and is most likely to engage the principal's empathy. The hope is that Benjamin will emerge from this entanglement with the knowledge he made an error, but has corrected it and need not feel personally diminished. Option A, of course, sounds legalistic, needlessly protectionist, and suggests lying is the appropriate policy. Option B is equally unsuitable. The parents' pride should not be the primary focus of this episode, nor their perception in the community. In this alternative, Benjamin would not gain social skill from the experience. Option D, of course, is an overreaction that the embarrassment is too much to handle and displays that the family has no confidence to sustain criticism. (See principles 3, 6, 8, 11.)

Scenario 7: A Conflict of Interest

It is near eighth-grade graduation at St. Anne's School, and every parent is proud of her child's achievements. In several months, some special awards will be presented on graduation night for outstanding achievement, and these awards can play a part in the selection of students for the local selective private high school in town. Hence, there is a lively competition for these awards, one of which is the Mackey Award, given to the eighth-grade girl who has demonstrated success in athletics while maintaining at least a 3.2 grade point average. St. Anne's is a small school, and everyone knows there are five girls who could win the Mackey. Laura, mother of one of the five girls, is on the two-person selection committee whose nomination goes to the athletic director who makes the final decision, and who will actually present the award on graduation night. Laura convinces the other committee member to adjust the selection criteria so that the girl candidate must have excelled in two sports, not just one. Not coincidentally, only her daughter, Carly, meets this newly established criteria, and therefore the other candidates would be eliminated. Jennifer, the mother of one of the other girls, hears of this shift in selection criteria and feels a sense of injustice, but she is conflicted that speaking up about it might ignite an awkward confrontation.

What do you advise Jennifer to do?

A. Present her objections to the selection committee and argue for maintaining the established criteria.

B. Appeal directly to the athletic director about this last-minute change in criteria and what it means for the other girls.
C. Ignore this situation as petty. In the long run it means nothing.
D. Work on other ways to acknowledge her daughter's achievement, which may be even better than recognition from the Mackey Award.

A Response to *A Conflict of Interest*

Parents are sometimes surprised to discover that other parents' competitive instincts can at times manifest themselves in manipulation and deception to promote the achievements of their children. Cheating at games or on exams and class projects can foster perversions in values and result in shameless self-promotion. The panel advised option B in the hope that the athletic director could rise above the mother in question's unchecked competitiveness. It is hoped that the director could discretely reestablish the selection process and reconsider multiple rather than single awards for these achievements. Option A might be possible, but it appears the two-person committee has already decided on their course, and it would be unlikely they would easily reconsider, especially if Laura's shameful behavior was made more obvious. Option C is possible, but it minimizes the present feelings of the girls. Option D is a good course that we hope parents would pursue regardless of these formal opportunities for recognition. As parents we continually look for opportunities for our children to experience success and learn that hard work and persistence have their rewards. And there should be enough positive recognition for everyone. (See principles 4, 5.)

Scenario # 8: Save the Last Dance for Me

Dick and Jan were parents of two girls, Nikki, age thirteen and Amy, age eleven. They were happy to transfer their daughters from the local public school to the highly regarded Trinity School, a private Christian school whose stated values were consistent with their own. The girls achieved good grades in its coed environment from the start, but they were all surprised to learn that in a month there would be a school-sponsored holiday dance. The custom was for boys to invite the girls, and soon a boy Amy liked in her seventh-grade class had invited her. Nikki, however, received no such offer and, to make matters worse, Nikki's two closest friends had been asked to the dance. Nikki was visibly disappointed and night after night retreated to her room often in muffled tears. Dick and Jan prayed that one of the boys would call to invite Nikki, but this time prayers were not enough to resolve Nikki's sense of rejection. Jan recalled her own sorrow of missing out on fun activities at school and asked Dick to "do something."

What would you advise Dick to do?

A. Give Nikki a pep talk—not attending this overrated affair would be no loss. Boys don't even dance but just stand around with their friends.

B. Unbeknownst to Nikki, Dick should call his golfing buddies and get one of their sons to invite Nikki to the holiday dance.

C. Identify the parents of boys and girls in Nikki's class whom he knew and whose children were not attending the dance and organize a get-together for them, and then drive them all as a group to the dance or an alternative event. It would be a group event without designated dates, and everyone who wanted could come.

D. Ignore it all and plan a family vacation to Disneyland.

A Response to *Save the Last Dance for Me*

One of the challenges of parenting is that even with the most sensitive listening and careful preparation for school subjects and events, there come along some events that are out of our control. When these involve feelings of acceptance and rejection, we realize we must proceed carefully to teach social skills as well as appropriate social behavior. This example raises the question: is it appropriate to have an invitational school dance in which there is a likelihood of exclusion and thus feelings of disappointment? Perhaps later in the school year, Dick and Jan, along with other parents, might discuss the wisdom of reframing this event for better inclusion and development of social skills. For the present dilemma, however, there can be some careful intervention which might not only respond to Nikki but to other girls (and boys too) in the same situation. Dick should consult with Nikki about the plan for a party or an event involving a number of friends and identify two or three other parents who support this idea, then consult with the school if they wish to attend the dance as a group. By bringing together a number of unattached students, it widens the participation and relieves some of the social pressure on them. It is even possible that the customs of this event could change. The panel therefore chose option C, even with the obvious social risks. Dick and Jan must be sure they have Nikki's support and find several other supportive parents who recognize increasing the opportunity to participate is the appropriate goal here. They may have to host the party themselves, but they should make it inclusive and a fun event for all. The panel felt a pep talk, option A, would not respond to Nikki's feelings of rejection, and option B, ignoring it, would similarly not address Nikki's feelings, which could be exacerbated by Amy's attendance. Option C could embarrass Nikki and obscure the realization that the customs of the holiday dance appear to require certain social skills prematurely. (See principles 1, 3, 4, 5.)

Scenario # 9: Till Death Do Us Part

Jeff and Sara had been married for nearly fifteen years, and both worked hard in their careers, he as a high school principal and she as a registered nurse. Their careers involved long days, and because of medical emergencies and irregular hours at the hospital, Jeff and Sara seldom had much time for themselves. Their two boys, Donnie, ten, and Danny, eight, needed a good deal of attention. Each boy was having difficulty in school and Danny had been diagnosed with ADHD. When the teachers' union disputed their contract, even Jeff's evenings were now stacked with meetings. Shortly thereafter, Sara was surprised to receive a call from Jim, her old high school boyfriend. He was divorced now and successful as a salesman whose territory took him through Sara's town. Sara was happy to hear from Jim, and his phone call awoke memories she thought she had forgotten. When he told her she was "the perfect woman" and had always thought so, Sara's heart warmed with nostalgia. Jim proposed they meet for a late lunch next week. He would be staying at the Marriott in town, and he knew the hotel had a good restaurant there. Sara thought she would like to see Jim.

What would you advise Sara to do?

A. Sara should meet Jim next week and renew old acquaintances. As they say, it's just lunch.
B. Sara should put him off. She is a married woman and she should not convey any impression that she has interest in old relationships.

C. Sara should meet for lunch and see how she feels about Jim and how he has changed. After all, he has come to realize she is the perfect woman he once passed up.

D. Sara should step back and assess her feelings of happiness to see Jim. What does it mean to her? How would Jeff feel about this meeting? Should she tell him about it? Before? After? At all?

A Response to *Till Death Do Us Part*

Do you remember the popular novel *The Bridges of Madison County*? Like many stories of a similar theme, it is appealing because we long for an intimacy that can help us escape the mundane realities of daily life. Everyone wants to feel a special love and admiration, and this is easier to achieve when we color the picture with fantasy. Jim has touched a suppressed need in Sara for loving attention and reawakened feelings from a time long ago when they had no burdens and responsibilities of career and family. Wouldn't it be good to return to such a state? Wouldn't it be nice to believe that Jim has finally realized what we all long to hear, that just the way we are is so valued that we deserve to be thought of as perfect? The reality, at some point, must intrude on this wishfulness, and the sooner the better. First, Sara has made a vow to love Jeff, so the reality of his existence cannot be ignored. It is likely Jeff would have some feelings about her meeting with an old boyfriend and predictable other feelings if he found out after the fact. In other words, Jeff and Sara are a couple, and this reality cannot be ignored. If either partner feels enticed by another person, this is a reflection of how they have allowed their relationship to lose its loving edge. This important realization calls for some kind of reflection as a couple, some attention to their life as a loving couple, and some awareness of its impact on their children. It is too easy to allow the tasks of daily life to erode our primary relationship, so we must realize that to succeed as a couple takes continuing work. Every day we read stories in the news of seductions where some intern or videographer says to the man, "You're so hot." Or some fellow woos a woman with the old line, "You are the perfect woman." Even Jerry Seinfeld had a humorous episode outlining a man's strategy of reciting such lines until there is an opening for advantage. It's a well worn phrase, but it still works when the woman is worn out and emotionally deprived. So the panel easily chose option D, where Sara should step back and examine her commitments. She needs to ask herself why she feels so glad to see Jim and how she feels about Jeff and her family. Self-understanding keeps us from impulsive mistakes. Option C sounds healthy but seems to be headed toward believing in her supposed perfection. Option B is cautious and perhaps needlessly so if Sara has gone through this aforementioned self-examination. Option A is simply naïve. Does anyone really think that lunch with an old girlfriend or boyfriend is merely lunch? Well, maybe it depends on the boyfriend or girlfriend. (See principle 12.)

Scenario 10: *Feelings of Rejection*

Roger and Rosemary were the thoughtful parents of five children—four boys and one girl. They quickly adapted to the culture of raising boys with their competitive instincts and aggressive approaches to problem solving. They felt successful in creating family harmony. Their youngest, Kristin, presented a different set of issues. She was a whiz academically and had made reliable friends up through sixth grade. But things changed in the seventh grade when the group of girls Kristin called friends began to display arbitrary decisions, rejections, and incomplete resolutions to hurt feelings among the girls. Even the parents noticed this capriciousness among the girls, but loyalties to their own daughters in the ebb and flow of social conflict prevailed. One day Kristin, who had recently been admitted to the gifted math section, told her mother that Emma, her best friend, was having a sleepover with their friends and had not invited her. Kristin felt hurt and rejected, and confused about this abrupt exclusion and looked to Rosemary for help.

What would you advise Rosemary to do?

A. Rosemary should call Emma's mother and try to get an invitation, however belated, for Kristin.
B. Rosemary should educate her daughter about the fickleness of young women and not trust them again.
C. Rosemary should organize a sleepover for Kristin and exclude Emma.
D. Rosemary should supportively explain how girls express aggression even for the pettiest reasons such as their own insecurities. It has little to do with Kristin and, it should not bring her down.

A Response to *Feelings of Rejection*

It is remarkable how many women recall the hurtful experiences of exclusion, rejection, or mean gossip. As noted in chapter 5, Rachel Simmons hit a nerve with her book *Odd Girl Out.* So the wise mother should prepare her daughter for these behaviors among girls. Since it is predictable, it would be wise to develop participation in alternative social groups, such as Kristin's church youth group and sports team. When some disruption in her school group occurs, such as her selection into the gifted math group, Kristin can find comfortable ground with another group ("social insurance"). In most cases these tensions are temporary and friends coalesce. In this case Rosemary talked it over with Kristin and decided to arrange an outing with friends from her church group. Agreeing with the need for girls to have several friendship groups, the panel chose option D. Option A would be an extreme course and may challenge Emma's mother's primary loyalty to her daughter, while possibly embarrassing Kristin. Learning how to trust in relationships can be an important lesson that will have implications later with girls as well as boys. So option B would be inappropriate. Finally, option C might sound supportive, even protective, but it prevents Kristin from learning to cope with these difficult feelings and will exacerbate the ambivalent feelings between the girls. (See principles 3, 5.)

Summing Up

I hope you found analyzing these scenarios beneficial and were able to put the principles we have discussed to the test. Score one point for each answer that was selected by our panel or award yourself a point for an answer you were able to defend using the principles described in preceding chapters. If you scored seven to ten points, congratulations! You are a master. If you scored four to six points, good going and look over the situations with which you experienced disagreement. Consult the preceding chapters for reference. If you scored less than four points, you may want to reread the main points of the book or discuss your viewpoints with your spouse. In any case, thank you for your interest in exploring the complexities of parenting. I wish you success in raising your sons and daughters, and if you would like to send me comments, questions, or issues for consultation on topics not covered in this book, feel free to send them to 12principlesofparenting.com.

Notes

Introduction

1. "Does Having Children Make You Unhappy?" Lisa Belkin, *New York Times*, April 1, 2009. This controversial article reports on research that posits that having children contributes to life's tensions. The majority of the blog responses point out that these are outweighed by the satisfactions children bring.

2. Paul T. Hill, "Equal Opportunity: Preparing Urban Youth for College," in *Hopes, Fears, and Reality: a Balanced Look at American Charter Schools in 2008*, ed. Robin J. Lake (Bothell, WA: University of Washington Center on the Reinvention of Public Education), pp-27–29.

3. I will refer to the significant adults in a child's life as parents, although I realize there are significant others who take on this vital role for many children.

4. Because most of these suggestions are aimed at both boys and girls, I will alternate pronouns for boys and girls. Unless otherwise stated, they will be interchangeable.

Chapter 1. Getting on the Right Track

1. Diana Baumrind, "Patterns of Parental Authority and Adolescent Autonomy" in *New Directions For Child Development: Changes in Parental Authority During Adolescence*, ed. J. Smetana (San Francisco: Jossey-Bass), pp. 61–69.

Chapter 2. Your Child's Growth and Development

1. Statistics and pediatric observations in this chapter are based on those used in "Physical Development Through Puberty," in *Caring for Your School-Aged Child: Ages 5-12*, ed. Edward Schor (New York: American Academy of Pediatrics, Bantam Books, 2004), pp. 3–16.

Chapter 3. Listening to Your Child

1. "Communicating With Your Child," in Schor, p. 197.
2. John Gottmann, *Raising the Emotionally Intelligent Child* (New York: Simon and Schuster, 1998), p. 127. Gottman advocates emotional coaching but advises caution under these circumstances.

Chapter 4. Collaboration with Your Child's School

1. Schor, "Getting Involved in Your Child's Schooling," p. 488. These are common questions the parent should ask. These questions and other topics are discussed in this chapter.

Chapter 5. A Note about Girls

1. Rachel Simmons, *Odd Girl Out: The Hidden Culture of Aggression in Girls* (New York: Harcourt Press, 2002). This book explores ways middle and junior high school girls develop and express angry feelings.
2. Carol Gilligan, *In a Different Voice: Psychological Theory and Women's Development* (Cambridge, MA: Harvard University

Press, 1982). Gilligan describes this concept, and it is further developed by JoAnn Deak in *Girls Will Be Girls* (New York: Hyperion Press, 2002), 232–42.

3. JoAnn Deak, PhD, *Girls Will Be Girls* (New York: Hyperion Press, 2002), 191–92. Deak presents a discussion of the importance of fathers on girls' emotional development.

Chapter 6. A Note about Boys

1. For an excellent discussion of raising boys, see *Raising Cain: Protecting the Emotional Life of Boys*, Dan Kindlon and Michael Thompson, (New York: Ballantine Books, 2000).

2. "Emotional intelligence" is Daniel Goleman's term in *Emotional Intelligence: Why It Can Matter More Than IQ* (New York: Bantam Books, 1995). John Gottman in *Raising an Emotionally Intelligent Child* (New York: Simon and Schuster, 1998), emphasizes "emotional coaching" the child. "Accurate empathy" is the generalized term, going back decades to Carl Rogers and others.

3. Kindlon and Thompson, 61.

4. Schor, "Changing Your Child's Behavior," 216.

5. Kindlon and Thompson, 96.

Chapter 7. The Harmonious Family: Siblings without Rivalry

1. For a thoughtful discussion of this topic, see *Siblings without Rivalry: How to Help Your Children Live Together So You Can Live Too* by Adele Faber and Elaine Mazlish (New York: Harper Perennial, 1998).

Chapter 8. Discipline as Teaching

1. These suggestions are made in Schor, "Changing Your Child's Behavior," 218–19. Other authors present similar cautions.

Chapter 9. Special Problems

1. For Further discussion on this topic, see Schor, "Managing Common Behavior Problems," 221–41.

2. This section written by Angela Celio Doyle, PhD, clinical associate at the University of Chicago in the department of psychiatry and behavioral neuroscience.

3. Dianne Neumark-Sztainer, *"I'm, Like, SO Fat!": Helping Your Teen Make Healthy Choices about Eating and Exercise in a Weight-Obsessed World* (New York: Guilford Press, 2005).

4. J. Fulkerson et al., "Family Dinner Meal Frequency and Adolescent Development: Relationships with Developmental Assets and High-Risk Behaviors, *Journal of Adolescent Health* 39, no. 3 (2006): 337–45.

5. James Lock and Daniel le Grange, *Help Your Teenager Beat an Eating Disorder*. New York: Guilford Press, 2005).

Chapter 11. Internet Safety

1. Amanda Lenhart,. *Teens and Social Media: An Overview*, April 10, 2009, Pew Internet & American Life Project. http://www.pewinternet.org/Presentations/2009/17-Teens-and-Social-Media-An-Overview.aspx.

Chapter 12. The Importance of Family

1. Courtney Jarchow, *Strengthening Marriage and Two-Parent Families* (Denver, CO: National Conference of State Legislatures, 2003), 2.

BOOK OF INTEREST

I Can Speak Bully

Kevin Morrison

Ages 4 to 8

A tool for parents to use in bringing their children on the journey of understanding bullies and how to help them find the friendship and acceptance they are truly looking for.

6744-9 $14.95 Hardcover

www.paulistpress.com

20 Tough Questions Teenagers Ask and 20 Tough Answers

Lois Leiderman Davitz and Joel R. Davitz

Answers to the tough questions in life that teenagers ask. No preaching, no rules, just rational responses to help teens cope with tough moral issues they face in life.

3807-7 $9.95 Paperback

www.paulistpress.com

BOOK OF INTEREST

Building a Family

A Handbook for Parenting with God

Marilyn Spaw Krock

A concise, God-centered treasure trove of simple, useful, often humorous suggestions for nurturing happy, healthy, faith-filled families.

4102-7 $14.95 Paperback

www.paulistpress.com

BOOK OF INTEREST

The Catholic Prayer Bible (NRSV)
Lectio Divina Edition

An ideal Bible for anyone who desires to reflect on the individual stories and chapters of just one, or even all, of the biblical books, while being led to prayer though meditation on that biblical passage.

0587-8 $39.95 Hardcover
4663-5 $29.95 Paperback
www.paulistpress.com

7-16

CPSIA information can be obtained at www.ICGtesting.com
Printed in the USA
LVOW08s1507230616

493837LV00001B/88/P